HISTORY

OF THE

FIRST COUNCIL OF NICE

A WORLD'S CHRISTIAN CONVENTION A.D. 325

WITH A LIFE OF CONSTANTINE

By

DEAN DUDLEY

ATTORNEY AT LAW

AND

MEMBER OF VARIOUS HISTORICAL SOCIETIES

HISTORY

OF THE

FIRST COUNCIL OF NICE

A WORLD'S CHRISTIAN CONVENTION A.D. 325

WITH A LIFE OF CONSTANTINE

By

DEAN DUDLEY

ATTORNEY AT LAW

AND

MEMBER OF VARIOUS HISTORICAL SOCIETIES

A&B Publishers Group
Brooklyn, New York
11238

manufactured in the United States.

ISBN 1-881316-03-3

COVER PHOTO
GIANT HEAD OF THE EMPEROR CONSTANTINE,
PART OF A STATUE FROM THE BASILICA OF
CONSTANTINE IN ROME.

CONTENTS

INTRODUCTION...7
LIFE OF CONSTANTINE 10

CHAPTER I
Prologue.— Objects and Results..23

CHAPTER II
The Date, and Sources of its History 25

CHAPTER III
The Causes which led Constantine to Convoke the Universal
Synod, commonly called "The General Council Of
Nice."..27

CHAPTER IV
Increase Of the Opposition to Arius and his Heresy.....................30

CHAPTER V
Letter of Arius to his friend, Eusebius of Nicomedia.
Describing his Doctrines, which Occasion the Opposition
and Severities of Alexander; and Letter of Eusebius of
Nicomedia, to Paulinus of Tyre, on the same Subject,
etc...38

CHAPTER VI.
The General Council of Nice—The Emperor Convokes the
Bishops from all Christendom..43

CHAPTER VII
The Countries which were Represented at the Universal
Synod.—Interesting Characters, Confessors, etc.,
Present.—Preliminary Disputations.—Three Distinct
Parties.—Arius Summoned.—Athanasius Appears....................46

CHAPTER VIII
Meeting of the Council in the Imperial Palace. —Presence
of Constantine.—His Splendid Appearances and
Speeches 54

CHAPTER IX

The Final Deliberation and Decisions of the Council upon the Important Questions of Doctrine. —Constantine Participates in The Debates.—The Arian Creed Rejected.—The Homoousian Established Forever. —Letters of the Council and Constantine, Describing the Unanimous Decisions Respecting the "Consubstantial" Creed. —Arius Anathematized And His Thalia Condemned; also the Arians Banished, and their Works Proscribed by the Emperor.. 59

CHAPTER X

The Pastoral Letter of Eusebius Pamphilus, of Cæsarea, Concerning the same Things, with Other Circumstances........ 67

CHAPTER XI

Accounts from Eustathius Concerning the Same Things; also from Athanasius, of Alexandria, as Quoted in Theodoret's History of the Church 73

CHAPTER XII

Disciplinary Laws Discussed. -—The Celibacy of the Clergy Proposed. —This Question Settled in Favor of Honorable Marriage. —Certain Canons Decreed And Established............ 79

CHAPTER XIII

The Letter Despatched from the Council Of Nice to the Church of Alexandria —Statement of What had been Decreed Against the Innovations Of Meletius, as well as the Council's Opinion of Arius and his Particular Heresies. 94

CHAPTER XIV

The Emperor's Kindness to the Bishops at the VICENNALIA.—His Entertainment of them.— He Kisses their Wounds.—His Munificence. — He Settles their Personal Difficulties in a Peculiar Way. — His Admonitions to Them.—Conclusion. —Epilogue. 99

CONSTANTINE THE GREAT.

INTRODUCTION.

The words *Council, Synod* and *Convention* are synonymous. There were many Councils held in Christendom before that of Nice; but they were not Œcumenical, that is, general or universal. At the first Councils the bishops probably represented only their several churches, but they gradually assumed more extensive powers, and claimed to represent larger districts.

In apostolic times the apostles chose the bishops; afterwards the disciples of the apostles chose them, subject to the approval of the community. After this age the bishops o f a province met together and appointed new bishops, which choice had to be ratified by the people. At the Council of Nice a new plan was adopted, as will be seen in the canons.

In the history of a single Council we shall obtain a glimpse of the condition of the Christian Church of that day, Constantine, the great emperor of Rome, being decidedly the most conspicuous figure in the picture. Therefore it seemed proper to add to this edition, his likeness, taken from a coin, and a sketch of his life. It is a pity that so splendid a man, both in form and courage, should have marred his record toward the end of life by inhuman acts of cruelty against his rivals and even his nearest relations. It don't seem possible that he could deem his baptism sufficient to wash out such stains and purify his soul. But he had heartless courtiers about him, who probably encouraged his pretensions to righteousness, and pandered to his vilest propensities.

He wished to convey the idea to his subjects that he felt sure of heaven; for he had a large gold coin struck, which represented, on one side, himself, partially concealed by a veil, and, on the other, his figure in a chariot, drawn by horses ascending to heaven, and a hand reaching down from the sky to receive him. I was somewhat amused to find, in an old Spanish work by Mexia, translated and published in London, A.D. 1604, the singular remarks of that author upon the last part of Constantine's life. He says that appearances are against the propriety of some of his acts, but then he found they must be all right, because St. Jerome and several other saints and popes had endorsed the great emperor as a good Christian and heir to eternal bliss. The modern Protestant writers are not so lenient towards him. How it happens that no Arian histories exist, I know not; unless it is because their enemies, the trinitarians, have destroyed them. It was the custom to punish heretics and burn their books in the very first days of Christian rule. Christianity, as an institution of the government, was little better than the old religion. It soon became transformed, so that Christ would have been ashamed of its name. As soon as there were fortunes to be made in the Church, it became the fruitful field of worldly ambition.

In regard to the Canons and Decrees: I think the best time for the Easter Festival would have been the ancient, honored day of the Jewish Passover. It was opposed merely by a whim of Constantine, because, as a Roman, he hated the nation which his country had long detested and persecuted, that is, the Jews, although he was forced to admit that God had ever preferred them before all other people. His change in the *Day of Rest* arose from the same unjust prejudice. The Sabbath was as good for Gentiles, as it had been for Israel; and, although Christ did not regard it as holy, he never appointed any other in its stead.

One of the canons forbids kneeling at prayers on Sundays. Dr. A. P. Stanley thinks this rule was adopted because the apostles used always to pray standing. But I suppose it was so ordered because Sunday was considered a day of triumph and rejoicing, not of humiliation. It was believed that on that day Christ rose from the dead, and conquered death and hell. Kneeling was a sign of submission to an enemy; therefore it was inappropriate for Sunday. It is strange no public prayers were offered at the Council. Another canon forbids the election of a eunuch to the office of bishop. To degrade manhood was deemed by some the best way to exalt their religion. Such folly needed to be discouraged by a stronger condemnation. Constantine showed the greatest respect to the confessors and ascetics. He put his lips to the scars received in persecution, and fancied he drew godliness from them.

Perhaps he did this to win the hearts of the good bishops. However, his superstition was equal to his cunning. He praised and patronized monks, nuns, hermits and devotees of every sort, who deprived themselves of the comforts of life, and despised nearly all social obligations. To live in rags and dirt, and eat herbs like some beasts was the holiest fashion in the estimation of the early Fathers. (They could not have deduced it from the life of Christ.) That kind of Christians, as well as martyrs, were often reputed to be workers of miracles.

No mention is made of the Bible being read publicly in the meetings of the "Great and Holy Synod," as it was called. St. Jerome said that he had heard from one of the fathers that the book of Judith was approved at Nicæa. But no other early writer mentions it. Historians often remark that the fathers had a way of interpreting Scripture different from ours, in these days. Constantine, in his "Oration to the Saints," speaks of the Garden of Eden as being located in some other world; and this was the belief of Tertullian and several other Christian writers, as Tatian, Clement of Alexandria, Origen, Jerome, &c. We can't help mistrusting the sincerity of some of the early Greek converts, who, immediately upon espousing the new religion, began to write books and sign the names of celebrated apostles or martyrs to their devout productions. The Epistle to the Hebrews, ascribed to Paul, is one of these. But it was so well done that many were willing to accept it as inspired. All the best critics say it cannot be Paul's writing, although it seems to contain his ideas, expressed by some other author.

The Apocalypse is another doubtful book. Modern criticism even rejects portions of the four evangelists. It would be remarkable that an unlettered Galilean, should have introduced into this book the Platonic "Logos," that is, "Word," just as the great philosopher used it, and laid the very bottom foundation of the Nicene creed. Does anyone nowadays undertake to prove that John, the disciple of Jesus, wrote that book, or even dictated it?

Then there was a work called the Shepherd of Hermas, that many early Christians took to be inspired; but they couldn't tell who was the author. It was made to sell to the faithful, simple souls, who looked only at the surface of such works. The story pleased them, being in saintly style, although a rather low style.

The Nicene fathers argued that the pagan religion was derived from the poets; and, therefore, was not of divine origin. But how could they deem that an objection, seeing that the prophets of the Old Testament were nearly all poets? And the most ancient religious books of various nations were sacred poems. It seems to me that faith and hope, which are considered the principal parts of religion, are peculiarly poetical themes. They are not scientific deductions, or historical facts. All men have capacity to enjoy them, whereas but few can comprehend or appreciate a logical argument, or even understand what is sufficient evidence to establish great theological dogmas. Most people must, therefore, necessarily found their belief upon the statements and practice of others; and such theories will be chosen, as are pleasing and flattering, whether in works of poetry or prose, provided they have been approved by custom and beloved forefathers. This disposition in mankind accounts for the tenacity with which many absurd principles are retained in institutions that have come down to us from the dark ages. It is the duty of science to dispel and discourage such things. Hence we often find the great savans, like Huxley and Tyndall, boldly opposing time-honored fallacies and false doctrines of the religious sects. The Council of Nice set the example of trying to compel Christians to adopt its modes of faith. That plan was not so fair as those pursued by the great philosophers. I suppose the Nicene fathers considered faith in Christ and the resurrection from the dead, as the fundamental doctrines of their religion. But there had been, as great and good religious teachers as they, who inserted no idea of a future state in their creeds: for instance, Moses and Confucius.

The great Hebrew author of Job makes him say:—

"I have made my bed in the darkness,
And where is now my hope?
As the waters fail from the sea,
And the flood decayeth and drieth up,
So man lieth down and riseth not."

Solomon, or another poet, in the same of that learned king, says:—

"For him that is joined to all the living there is hope,
For a living dog is better than a dead lion.
The living know that they shall die,
But the dead know not anything,
Neither have they any more a reward.
All things come alike to all,
This is an evil among all things
That are done under the sun,
That there is one event unto all.
There is one event to the righteous and to the wicked."
—*Eccles.*

The Israelites had no belief, at this time, in an incorporeal soul, any more than the Egyptians had in the time of Moses. They believed in ghosts.

But one of our English poets sings,—

"Religion! Providence! an after state!
Here is firm footing; here is solid rock!
His hand the good man fastens on the skies,
And bids Earth roll, nor feels her idle whirl.
Poor mutilated wretch that disbelieves!
By dark distrust his being cut in two,
In both parts perishes; life void of joy,
Sad prelude of eternity in pain!"
—*Young*

Whether Jesus taught the doctrine of an eternal hell for punishment in the after life, is question among doctors of divinity. Origen denied it. The Roman Catholic Church has adopted purgatory in imitation of the *sheol, hades* or *tartarus.* That church has many doctrines, forms and rites similar to those of the older religions. Jesus seems to have considered doing good deeds and living a pure life the true way to worship God.

LIFE OF CONSTANTINE.

Constantine the Great, born A.D. 274, was named Constantine, Caius Flavius Valerius Aurelius Claudius. His father was Constantine Chlorus[1] and the mother, his wife Helena.[2] Being the eldest son, Constantine, soon after the death of his father, in 306, was proclaimed emperor by the troops, and in 307 married Fausta, the daughter of Maximian; but Eusebius says that God, the supreme governor of the world, by his own will, appointed Constantine to be prince and sovereign.

"It is my intention," continues Eusebius, "to pass over very many of the deeds of this thrice-blessed prince, as, for example, his conflicts and engagements in the field, and his triumphs, and to speak and write of those circumstances only which refer to his religious character."

The father of Constantine had three colleagues in the government, Diocletian,[3] Maximian[4] and Galerius,[5] all of whom persecuted the Christians; but he was the friend of the Christians' God, and devoted to the love of Christ.

---

[1] He was a son of Eutropius, a nobleman of Dardania, in Mœsia, and his wife, Claudia, a niece of the Emperor Claudius, of the Flavian line. The designation, "Chlorus," was given him on account of the paleness of his complexion.

[2] Helena was the daughter of an inn-keeper at Drepanum, in Sicily.

[3] The parents of Diocletian had been slaves in the house of Anulius, a Roman senator. He became a soldier, and gradually rose, on account of his great talents, till he arrived at the imperial throne. "His reign was more illustrious," says Gibbon, "than that of any of his predecessors."

[4] Marcus Valerius Maximian, of obscure parentage, was named by Diocletian, his colleagues in the Roman Empire, A.D. 286. Put to death by order of Constantine, at Marseilles, A.D. 310. He was the father of Fausta, second wife of Constantine. His first wife was Minervina, of obscure family. We are not told what became of her.

[5] Galerius was a herdsman in his youth. He assumed the name of Valerius, and is called also Armentarius. He was a brave general, and was raised by Diocletian to the title of Cæsar, and married Valeria, daughter of Diocletian.

Constantine, soon after coming into power, resolved to destroy his colleague, Maxentius,[1] who adhered to the old idolatry; but he felt the need of some more powerful aid than his army, especially on account of the wicked and magical enchantments which were so diligently practiced by the tyrant. Therefore he began to seek for divine assistance.

What particularly confirmed him in this course was the recollection that his father, who had opposed the persecuting spirit of his colleagues, and honored the one Supreme God during his whole life, had found him to be the Saviour and Protector of his empire.

"Accordingly," says Eusebius, "he called on him, with earnest prayer and supplications, that he would reveal to him who he was, and stretch forth his right hand to help him in his present difficulties. And, while he was thus praying with fervent entreaty, a most marvellous sign appeared to him from heaven, the account of which it might have been difficult to receive with credit, had it been related by any other person.

"But since the victorious emperor himself, long afterwards declared it to the writer of this history, when he was honored with his acquaintance and society, and confirmed his statement by an oath, who could hesitate to credit the relation, especially since the testimony of after-time has established its truth? He said that about midday, when the sun was beginning to decline, he saw with his own eyes the trophy of a cross of light in the heavens, above the sun, and bearing the inscription: 'IN HOC SIGNO VINCES!' *'Under this sign thou shalt conquer.'*

"At this sight he himself was struck with amazement, and his whole army also, which happened to be following him on some expedition, and witnessed the miracle.

"He moreover said, that he doubted within himself what the import of this apparition could be. And while he continued to

---

[1] Maxentius was son of Maximian, and was proclaimed Emperor at Rome, A.D. 306. He fell at the battle of the Milvian Bridge, A.D. 312, fighting against Constantine. He was a vile tyrant, but not a persecutor. *Milman. Gibbon says (year* 312), Constantine , after the victory over Maxentius, put to death his two sons, and carefully extirpated his whole race.

ponder and reason on its meaning, night imperceptibly drew on; and in his sleep the Christ of God appeared to him with the same sign which he had seen in the heavens, and commanded him to procure a standard made in the likeness of that sign, and to use it as a safeguard in all engagements with his enemies.

"At dawn he set his artificers to work, and had the signal made and beautified with gold and gems. The Romans now call it the 'Labarum.' It was in the following form: A long spear overlaid with gold, crossed by a piece, laid over it. On the top of all was a crown, formed of gold and jewels interwoven, on which were placed two letters indicating the name of Christ; the Greek letter P being intersected by X exactly in its centre. From the transverse piece, which crossed the spear, was suspended a banner of purple cloth covered with profuse embroidery of bright jewels and gold. It was of square form, and over it (beneath the cross) was placed a golden half-length picture of the emperor and his children. This standard he ordered to be carried at the head of all his armies."

Eusebius often calls it the "saving signal," the "salutary symbol," the "salutary trophy," &c., and he moreover says the emperor told him that none of those who bore this standard ever received a wound. All the enemies' darts would stick in the spear and not touch the bearer. It is singular that Eusebius seemed to believe all the miracles Constantine ever narrated, and they were numerous.

It is said in Mosheim's Ecclesiastical History, that Eusebius was probably mistaken in regard to the emperor's vision being really seen by him; because the sign of the cross had long been used by the Christians; and it is more reasonable to suppose that Constantine only *dreamed* that he saw it in the heavens, as he described, with the inscription about conquering.

Eusebius is sometimes blamed for his adulation of this hero. In one place he says, God himself was present to aid him all through his reign, "holding him up to the human race as an exemplary pattern of godliness."

The first tyrant to be destroyed was Maxentius, who had been exceedingly wicked, but "his crowning point was having recourse to sorcery." When this colleague was overthrown,

Constantine sang: "Who is like to Thee, O Lord, among the gods?" Then the victor set up his statue in Rome, holding in his hand the Labarum, with this inscription engraved upon it: "By virtue of this salutary sign, which is the true symbol of valor, I have preserved and liberated your city from the yoke of tyranny," &c.

The Christian ministers at Rome[1] were treated with great distinction, and all who had been imprisoned or banished were released or recalled. Costly offerings were made to the churches, and the poor were relieved, even from the emperor's private funds.

The next tyrant to be destroyed for his crimes and impiety was Maximian, "who was detected in a treasonable conspiracy," and after him others of the same family, "all their intentions being miraculously revealed by God through visions to his servant. For he frequently vouchsafed to him manifestations of himself, the divine presence appearing to him in a most marvellous manner, and giving to him many intimations of future events."

The third tyrant was Licinius, who had married the sister of Constantine. This colleague also "employed himself in machinations against his superior, and resolved at last to carry arms against God himself, whose worshipper he knew the emperor to be."

Licinius had forbidden women to receive instruction from the bishops, or even visit the churches with men, "directing the appointment of females to be the teachers of their own sex, and devised other means for effecting the ruin of the churches." The fourth tyrant, Galerius Valerius, ruler of the Eastern provinces, who stood in the way of Constantine, had a fatal disease overtake him, as a judgment from God. And he was loaded with an enormous quantity of fat, from gluttony. A vast number of worms swarmed in him, because he had persecuted Christians, and engaged in battle relying upon demons, whom he wor-

---

[1] Stanley says, Constantine, doubtless, gave the Palace of the Lateran to Silvester Bishop of Rome, and this was beginning of the papal ascendency. This palace had been the estate of Fausta, the wife of the emperor.

shipped as gods. Maximin,[1] and his children, were destroyed, A.D. 313, by Licinius.

Licinius, after some years of peaceful rule in Thrace, Asia, Minor, Syria, and Egypt, became engaged in other conflicts with Constantine, and, being taken prisoner, was put to death by his conqueror, together with his supporters.

Then Constantine adopted the title of "Victor," and so governed the Roman empire alone.

The exiled and enslaved martyrs were released, the confessors honored, and confiscated estates restored to the proper owners or heirs.

Laws were promulgated forbidding anyone to erect images or practice divination, or offer sacrifices in any way in their private houses; churches were ordered to be built, and old ones to be repaired and enlarged. At this time the heathen temples were not closed or suppressed.

Great dissensions had arisen in the church of Egypt about the nature of Christ, and the time to celebrate Easter, by which Constantine was much troubled. He therefore ordered a convention to be held at Nicæa in Bithynia, to which bishops were invited from all parts of the world, hoping that harmony might result from the decision of such a Universal Assembly of the chief Christians of the world.

After these questions had been decided, the emperor directed his attention to building a great church at Jerusalem, on the spot where it was supposed the Holy Sepulchre had been discovered. The old cave was cleared of rubbish, and the most magnificent church in the world erected over it.

---

[1]   There were six sovereigns of the Roman Empire, A.D. 308, namely. Galerius, Maximian, Constantine, Maxentius, Licinius, and Maximin. Of these, Constantine alone survived at the time of the council of Nice. Only one of them had died a natural death; i.e., Galerius, in 311. Maximin was conquered by Licinius, and fled to Tarsus, where he is said to have been poisoned in 313. His name was Maximin Daia, or Daza, and he had been an Illyrian peasant, being made Cæsar by Galerius, who was a relative. A.D. 303.

Helena Augusta,[1] Constantine's aged mother, visited Palestine and built a church at Bethlehem, and another on the Mount of Olives. She gave many presents to the poor, released prisoners, did many acts of kindness, mingling with the ordinary worshippers in modest attire, and exhibited a true Christian spirit. She died in her eightieth year, in presence of the emperor. Her likeness was impressed on golden coins.

Now, at last, Constantine began to abolish idolatry at Constantinople, and to build churches there and in Nicomedia, &c. At this command the heathen temples and images were everywhere destroyed. In all his orders respecting church affairs, he acted like an ancient pope. Heresies were cursed and condemned, and heretics deprived of their right of holding meetings, and their houses of prayer were bestowed on the Catholic Church. Their books he ordered to be sought for and destroyed.

Constantine had his likeness represented on golden coins, with the eyes uplifted, in the attitude of prayer.

And our present legal institution of Sunday was established by this man's authority. "He enjoined on all the subjects of the Roman empire to observe the Lord's Day as a day of rest."

This decree for the general observance of Sunday[2] appears to have been issued A.D. 321, before which time both "the old and new Sabbaths" were observed by Christians. Gibbon says he called the Lord's Day *"Dies solis,"* that is, the *Day of the Sun,*

---

[1]   Augusta was her title, probably bestowed by Constantine. Maximian, when he made Constantius-Chlorus "Cæsar," required him to divorce Helena, and marry his wife's daughter, Theodora. At this time, Constantine was eighteen years old.   Helena, while in Palestine, discovered the Holy Sepulchre and the true cross, and superintended the building of the great church at Jerusalem, over the Holy Sepulchre, as well as others in the Holy Land.

[2]   It was not generally called "Sunday" before this time; probably, never so called.   Constantine had claimed Apollo, the sun-god, as his patron, and even after becoming a Christian he stamped Apollo's image on one side of his coin, and the initials of Christ on the other.   The earlier Fathers of the Church observed the first day of the week as a day of rejoicing and triumph, because Christ, on that day, triumphed over the grave, and initiated the resurrection.   They did not wholly cease from labor, but observed the old Sabbath as a day of rest.   The first day of the week was, by them, called the "Lord's Day."

or *Sun'sday.* "This day," he said, "should be regarded as a special occasion for prayer." And he gave his soldiers the following form of prayer to use: "We acknowledge thee the only God; we own thee as our King, and implore thy succor. By thy favor we have gotten the victory: through thee are we mightier than our enemies. We render thanks for thy past benefits, and trust thee for future blessings. Together we pray to thee, and beseech thee long to preserve to us, safe and triumphant, our Emperor Constantine and his pious sons." He encouraged celibacy, of the old virgin stamp, having a great veneration for it.

In the thirtieth year of his reign, his great Church of the Holy Sepulchre having been founded, he wished to dedicate it in a becoming manner; and therefore he directed that the bishops who had assembled at the Synod of Tyre in Phœnicia, should be conveyed from there to Jerusalem as soon as they were ready to go; and most of them went to attend the dedication. It was the greatest synod of bishops, after that of Nicæa, that had ever assembled. There were present prelates from all the Roman provinces in Europe, Asia, and Africa. Eusebius says he was there and delivered several orations. He also shortly afterwards went to Constantinople and delivered another oration in the emperor's presence. About this time (A.D. 330) he founded Constantinople.[1]

Constantine continued to build churches and compose religious discourses up to his last days. In the thirty-first year of his reign, and the sixty-third of his age, he fell sick, and desired the bishop where he was, in Nicomedia, to baptize him, which was done; and he thought this ceremony had the effect to purify and purge his soul from past errors. He put on white robes, refusing to wear purple any more, made some noble bequests, and died on the last day of the feast of Pentecost, May 22, 337. His body was laid in a golden coffin in the great Church of the Apostles at Constantinople, which he had built and designed for his sepulchre.

---

[1] "Of all the events of his life," says Dean Stanley, "this choice is the most convincing and enduring proof of his real genius. No city, chosen by the art of man, has been so well chosen, and so permanent."

The religious belief of this wonderful man is a matter of deep interest. His theories are expressed in his own words, and his faith we may know by his deeds.

In a great oration[1] addressed by him to the Assembly of the Saints, he declares that Providence rules all things like fate; that justice is ever done, and that men receive here what they merit from Heaven's almighty ruling hand. His precise words are,—

"The events which befall men are consequent upon the tenor of their lives. Pestilence, sedition, famine, and plenty are all regulated with reference to our course of life."[2]

In regard to the philosophers who search into the secrets of nature, he remarks, that they often obscure the truth, when the subject of their reasoning surpasses their powers. So Socrates played constantly with the subtleties of controversy. And Plato, although he was sound in asserting that the word (logos) is God, and also the Son of God, yet he errs by introducing a plurality of gods. Pythagoras lied when he said that his knowledge came directly as a revelation from God, for he received it from the Egyptian priests.

"The soul of man is eternal," says Constantine; "but all things which had a beginning must have an end."

The coming of Christ, he asserts, was predicted by the prophets, the sibyls, and sublime poets. Even Virgil refers to the Christians where he sings,—

"Behold a new, a heaven-born race appears."
And again,—
"Begin, Sicilian Muse, a loftier strain,
The voice of Cuma's oracle is heard again."

"See where the circling years new blessings bring;
The virgin comes, and He, the long-wished king."

"Beneath whose reign, the iron offspring ends,—
And golden progeny from Heaven descends."

---

[1] The emperor used to preach in his palace halls to thousand of people, who would gather there out of curiosity to hear him.

[2] He trusted in Providence, like Cromwell, and had a standing army of 300,00 men, and twenty-nine naval squadrons.

"His kingdom banished Virtue shall restore,
And Crime shall threat the guilty world no more."
—*See Dryden's Virgil, Ecl.* 4.

The emperor had great faith in prayer. He says, "The righteous prayer is thing invincible, and no one fails to attain his object who addresses holy supplication to God." He believed in a judgment and future punishment for the wicked.

The principal faults of this founder of the Christian power in Rome were, according to Mosheim. Gibbon and other historians, very similar to those of our English sovereign Henry VIII., founder of the Protestant ascendency in Great Britain. He was wilfull, voluptuous, and self-conceited. His heart was capable of extreme cruelty, as shown by his acts toward several of his near relatives.[1] Even a son, named Crispus, fell a victim to his jealous resentment.[2] He assumed that he was born to reign, and held his commission from God. The flattery of the prelates might have augmented this conceit; for it was sometimes excessively fulsome.

Eusebius says, that on one occasion a Christian orator asserted, in the emperor's presence, that he would share the Empire of Heaven with Christ in the world to come. *See Life of Constantine, book IV. chap. 48; English translation of 1845 (anonymous), which I have often quoted.*

---

[1] Gibbon says, that, after Constantine had put his wife's father to death, in Gaul, he gained a victory over the Franks and Allemanni, and gave their chiefs to be devoured by wild beasts in the public ampitheatre of Treves. Another historian says, a great number of the French youth were also exposed to the same cruel and ignominious death. "Yet," says Gibbon, "his reign in Gaul, excepting his destruction of Maximian, seems to have been the most innocent and even virtuous period of his life."

[2] Julian charged his uncle, Constantine, who was also the father of his wife, with being "a voluptuary, a profligate and a murderer." Dean Stanley says, he put to death five of his near relatives, one being his wife, Fausta, and one, an eleven-year old son of Licinus and his wife Constantia, Constantine's half-sister.

Constantine favored the Arians very much in some parts of his life, under the influence of Eusebius of Nicomedia, by whom he was baptized and other Arian courtiers.

Constantine was peculiar in his dress, looks, and manners. In his later days he had a red complexion, and somewhat bloated appearance. His eyes were bright, and glared like those of a lion. His neck was thick, his voice soft and gentle.

The spear of the soldier was ever in his hand, and a helmet on his head, studded with jewels, and bound round with the Oriental diadem. He wore it on all occasions. His robe, of imperial purple or scarlet, was made of silk, richly embroidered with pearls and flowers, worked in gold. He took much care of his hair, at last wearing wigs of false hair, of various colors. His beard was shorn like that of the early Cæsars. His appetite was voracious, gluttonous. His wit was crisp and dry. He never lost his presence of mind.—*Stanley.*

Gibbon says of him: "In Constantine we may contemplate a hero, who so long inspired his subjects with love, and his enemies with terror, degenerating into a cruel and dissolute monarch, corrupted by his fortune, or raised by conquest, above the necessity of dissimulation. His old age was disgraced by the vices of rapaciousness and prodigality, and he lost the esteem of his subjects."

The emperor had been twice married. His first wife was Minervina, of obscure family, who bore him the son, Crispus. The brothers of Constantine were Julius Constantius, Dalmatius, and Hannibalianus,[1] this last-named having no children. Gallus and Julian were sons of Julius Constantius: and Dalmatius had two sons, named Dalmatius and Hannibalianus. Crispus was an amiable and accomplished youth. Eusebius, the historian, calls him a "brave and pious son." He had been engaged in his father's wars since 17 years of age, and had the deserved esteem and admiration of the court, the army and the people. "This dan-

---

[1] These three were brothers only by being sons of his father. Their mother was Theodora, the second wife of Chlorus. She was also the mother of Constantia, who married Licinius, and was a woman of great abilities and kindness of heart. Constantia belonged to the Arian sect, and had Eusebius of Nicomedia for her spiritual adviser.

gerous popularity," says Gibbon, "Soon excited the attention of Constantine, who, both as a father and as a king, was impatient of an equal." He was confined almost as a prisoner to his father's court, and exposed, without power of defence, to the calumny of his enemies. The emperor began to hint at suspicions of a conspiracy against his person and government. By rewards he invited informers to accuse even his most intimate favorites. The adherents of Crispus were the victims chosen. Constantine soon ordered him to be apprehended and killed, and the only son[1] of Constantia, the emperor's sister, in spite of her prayers and tears, shared the same fate. She did not long survive this blow, dying A.D. 329.

The church historian, Eusebius, first orator at the Nicene Council, no where mentions these horrible scenes in his prince's life. Other writers say that Fausta was the instigator of the murder of her stepson, Crispus. And they say Constantine so much repented of his cruelty, that he had her killed soon after, by being suffocated in a boiling hot bath. Philostorgius says the emperor murdered two wives, and that his three sons, who succeeded him were the sons of an adulteress. He declares that Fausta was innocent. Helena, the aged mother of Constantine, lamenting the fall of Crispus, soon revenged it; and Fausta was accused of adultery with a slave.[2] Her condemnation quickly followed; although she and Constantine had been husband and wife for twenty years, and had four daughters[3] and three sons, viz., Constantine, Constantinus, and Constans, who became heirs to the Roman empire. Gibbon suggests some doubt about Fausta being destroyed. She was murdered privately in the imperial palace, if at all. "Chrysostom, the orator, indulges his fancy by

---

[1]   This boy's name was Licinius, aged eleven years. He had the title of Cæsar.

[2]   Or soldier of the Imperial Guard. But it was, probably, a false charge. Fausta's death occurred, A.D. 327. Helena died 328. Crispus and his friends were put to death in 326.

[3]   Constantine's four daughters were: 1, Constantia, wife of Hannibalianus, son of Dalmatius, half-brother to the emperor; 2, Constantina, 3, Flavia Maxima, wife of Gratian, the son of Valentinian; 4, Helena, wife of Julian, son of the emperor's half-brother Constantius.

exposing the naked empress on a desert mountain to be devoured by wild beasts."

Mosheim says, "Constantine's life was not such as the precepts of Christianity required." He put to death his own son, and his wife Fausta, on a groundless suspicion, and cut off his brother-in-law Licinius and the unoffending son of Licinius, contrary to his plighted word. Nevertheless, the Greek Church has canonized him, and adores the memory of St. Constantine.—*J.R. Schlegel.*

After his death, the bishop, to whom his will had been entrusted for Constantius, brought out a document as the will,[1] which represented that the brothers and nephews of the late emperor had attempted to poison him, and directing that his death should be avenged on them. Whereupon the soldiers declared they would have no sovereigns but the sons of Constantine; and, Constantius probably conniving at the crime, his two uncles and several cousins, with some of their friends, were murdered in cold blood.—*Gibbon.*

Constantine was not a great man in depth and penetration of intellect, but exceedingly shrewd, prompt, and energetic in all the affairs of life, and inspired by such unbounded selfish ambition, that he overcame difficulties, which far greater souls would have deemed insurmountable. His credulity and superstition, which arose probably from ignorance of even the first principles of natural science, were the only checks upon his evil propensities. And both the old religion and the new, as he understood them, taught that every event was a special providence, and Jehovah, or some other deity, was the first and only cause of all our fortunes. However, according to his plan, sovereigns were instruments to carry on the affairs of the world, so they might imitate the Heavenly King, and make laws for nations, slay their subjects at pleasure, as the laws of nature do, and wield the sword and fire, and every kind of vengeance, against their foes, without overstepping the bounds of their proper sphere; and whatever

---

[1] The will was confided to a chaplain, who gave it to Eusebius of Nicomedia, and this bishop not liking to keep it in his hands, put it into the hand of the dead Emperor, where Constantius found it.—*Stanley Philostorgius.*

God allowed to be successful, bore the stamp of his approval, inasmuch as it would not have been permitted unless it were right.

He was taught by the bishops that God sent his only Son to be crucified for the benefit of mankind; therefore a sovereign might order his son to be sacrificed for the good and peace of society. Under the influence of such fanaticism, he perhaps committed all his bloody crimes without feeling their real enormity. But his character and influence cast a dark shade over the Christianity which he established.

"It is one of the most tragical fact of all history," says John Stuart Mill, "that Constantine, rather than Marcus Aurelius, was the first Christian Emperor. It is a bitter thought how different the Christianity of the world might have been, had it been adopted as the religion of the empire under the auspices of Marcus Aurelius, instead of those of Constantine."—*Essay on Liberty*, p. 58.

Dr. Stanley, of the Episcopal Church, gives some pointed, finishing touches to this sketch. He says the horrors of Constantine's domestic life, which he tried in vain to conceal, occurred about the time he conquered Maxentius. While he was at Rome, an inscription was found one day over the gates of the Palatine, catching at his weak points, Oriental luxury, and cruelty:—

> "*Saturni aurea sæcla quis requirit?*
> *Sunt hæc gemmea, sed Neroniana.*"

Which I translate,—

> "The golden times of Saturn, who'd restore?
> Ours shine with gems, *but Nero reigns once more.*"

Hosius, the emperor's counsellor in the West, came to Rome about the time with Helena, and relieved him of his deep distress, by assuring him that there are no sins so great, but in Christianity they may find forgiveness.

The emperor has been charged with a great many crimes besides these, which are proved. He was said to have sought absolution from the pagan priests, and even had an infant sacrificed and its entrails examined at the suggestion of a Jew. Many suspicions and legends against him are quoted at length by both heathen and Christian historians.

THE FIRST ŒCUMENICAL

COUNCIL OF NICE

CHAPTER I

The principal object of this famous Synod was to discuss and settle, upon a firm basis, the true Christian doctrine respecting the Divine nature of Christ, and his precise relation to the Almighty Deity of the material Universe; because the churches, and even the public, had been recently disquieted by the Arian controversy. But there were other questions of doctrine and discipline to be determined by this great Assembly of Christian Prelates; the more prominent of which questions were those relating to the Meletians, for having agitated a novel dogma, and the Novatians, for the same reason, and the most appropriate day for celebrating the Passover.

Constantine the Great, the first Christian emperor of the Roman World,[1] having been appealed to by some of the most noted bishops to take cognizance of these affairs of the church, being now relieved from his political antagonists, conceived and executed the design of summoning the Council of Nice; in which Synod he might exert all his influence to effect a reconciliation among the contentious prelates and churches, as

---

[1] Dr. Mosheim says,—"About A.D. 313, Constantine, who had been previously a man of no religion, is said to have embraced Christianity. But he also regarded some other religions as likewise true and useful to mankind." His purpose of abolishing the ancient religion of the Romans, and of tolerating only the Christian religion, he did not disclose till a little while before his death; when he published his edicts for pulling down the Pagan temples, and abolishing the sacrifices. According to the historian Zosimus (lib. ii., p. 104), an Egyptian (probably Hosius, bishop of Cordova in Spain), came to Rome and instructed the emperor upon the nature of Christianity.

well as conciliate their favor, and unite all in support of his character and his dominion.

These objects were all attained by means of the Council, except the principal one. Arianism, though checked for a short time, again burst forth with tenfold energy, and long agitated the religious world.[1] However, it finally was completely vanquished and eradicated from the high places of Christendom. And the Synod of Nice, on account of its antiquity, its universality, and its princely splendor, as well as the magnitude of its deliberations, as it had no precedent, so it has no equal in ecclesiastical history.[2]

---

[1] The Arian sect, for three hundred years, were a great power. The Goths and Teutons, Alaric, Genseric, Theodoric, and the Lombards were all Arians.

[2] The Roman Catholic Church recognizes twenty General Councils,—the *first* A.D. 50, the *second*, 325, at Nicæa, and the *last*, 1870; but there was no general council held in the year 50, according to the vest authorities, so that the Council of Nice was unquestionably the first that was ever convened, and certainly it is the most celebrated in the whole history of the Christian Church.

ŒCUMENICAL COUNCILS.

1. Nicæa, ... A.D. 325	11. Third of Lateran, . 1179
2. First Constantinople	12. Fourth of Lateran, 1215
3. Ephesus, ... 431	13. First of Lyons, 1245
4. Chalcedon, . . . 451	14. Second of Lyons, 1274
5. Second Constantinople, 553	15. That of Vienna, 131
6. Third Constantinople, 680	16. Constance, 1414-18
7. Second Nicæa, ... 787	17. Basle, 143.
8. Fourth Constantinople, 869	18. Fifth Lateran, 1512-17
9. First of Lateran, ... 1123	19. Trent, 1545-63
10. Second of Lateran, ... 1139	20. Council of the Vatican, 1870

CHAPTER II

THE DATE, AND SOURCES OF ITS HISTORY.

This Council was convened at the city of Nicæa, in the Roman province Bithynia, a country of Asia, lying between the Propontis and Black Sea, in the six hundred and thirty-sixth year from the commencement of Alexander the Great's reign and A.D. 325, the twentieth year of the reign of Constantine the Great, and in the consulate of Paulinus and Julian of Rome. The transactions of the Council are related by the ancients in a partial, imperfect, and disjointed manner, as I will briefly show by quoting several of the varying statements of its precise date, although there is no discrepancy respecting the year. Socrates Scholasticus[1] says, "It was *convened* on the twentieth day of May." But the Emperor had assigned the tenth day before the nones of June, that is, the 25th May, as I glean from Baronius' Annals of the Church, tome IV, and Baronius says it terminated on the 25th August, A.D. 325. The date of the Formulary, or Confession of Faith, established by the Council, and found prefixed to that document, is the nineteenth day of June, A.D. 325.[2] A letter from Hosius, and others of the Council, to Silvester, the Roman pope, bears date as I find in Baronius, thus: "VIII. Kalen. Julias;" that is, the eighth day before the first of July. Finally, the

---

[1] Socrates, surnamed Scholasticus, or the Advocate, that is, the Lawyer, while practicing law at Constantinople, compiled a History of the Church, from the accession of Constantine, A.D. 305, to the thirty-eighth year of Theodosius II., including a period of about 140 years. I quote from Bohn's edition, translated from the Greek. This author was born at Constantinople about A.D. 379, and received his education in that city. [*See the notice of Hermias Sozomen, in another note.*] He was a favored of the Novatian Sect, which was Trinitarian, but slightly heretical, as he admits, although the heresy consisted in a matter of discipline; the Novatians (so called from Novatus, a Roman presbyter, who had separated himself from the church) contending that those who, in times of persecution, had lapsed from the faith, should not be allowed a place for restoration.—*See Lardner's Cabinet Cyc., i., 133.*

[2] It is the same in the Greek collection of the canons.

very learned ecclesiastical historian, Dr. Augustus Neander, asserts that the *assembling* of the great Synod must have been as late as July. This last mentioned writer points out, in his following excellent observation, the plan I shall endeavor to pursue in this work, when he says,—"As no complete collection of the transactions of this Council [of Nice][1] has come down to us, the only means left, for obtaining a knowledge of the true course of its proceedings, is to take the accounts given by those reporters of the different parties, who were present at the deliberations, and form our conclusions from a comparison of them all." I shall also give some additional narratives of persons and important events connected with the history of the Nicene Council and its decrees; quoting the oldest and best authorities, and not always noting the omissions, which will be made for the sake of brevity.

I shall be cautious of judging the motives of the partisans in this Council, but let the reader form his own conclusions from facts and actual transactions and attendant circumstances. There is manifest partiality in all the original accounts, from which these facts and circumstances are to be gleaned. "The Arian history needs," says Dr. Murdock, in his translation of Mosheim, "a writer of integrity, and void alike of hatred and love."

---

[1] The words interpolated by me always be thus included in brackets.

CHAPTER III.

THE CAUSES WHICH LED CONSTANTINE TO CONVOKE THE UNIVERSAL SYNOD, COMMONLY CALLED "THE GENERAL COUNCIL OF NICE."

After the death of the wicked tyrants, Maxentius, Maximin, and Licinius, says Theodoret,[1] the storm abated which their atrocity, like a furious whirlwind, had excited against the church. The hostile winds were hushed, and tranquillity ensued. This was effected by Constantine, a prince deserving of the highest praise; who, like the divine apostle, was not called by man, or through man, but by God. He enacted laws prohibiting sacrifices to idols, and commanding churches to be erected. He appointed believers to be the governors of the provinces, ordered that honor should be shown to the priests, and threatened with death those who dared to insult them.

The churches which had been destroyed were rebuilt; and others, still more spacious and magnificent than the former ones, were erected. Hence the concerns of the church were smiling and prosperous, while those of her opponents were involved in disgrace and ruin. The temples of the idols were closed; but frequent assemblies were held, and festivals celebrated, in the churches. . . . . . .

At this time Peter was bishop of Alexandria, a large and populous city, and considered the metropolis, not only of Egypt, but also of the adjacent countries, Thebes and Libya. After Peter, the illustrious champion of the faith, had, during the sway of wicked tyrants, obtained the crown of martyrdom, the Church of

---

[1] This Christian historian, whose text I intend to quote as well as his idea, was born at Antioch, in Syria, about A.D. 387, and died about A.D. 458. He was bishop of Cyrus in his fatherland: although at one time a Nestorian, on account, probably, of his personal friendship for Nestorius, who rejected the title— "Mother of God"—as it was applied to the Virgin Mary. But he renounced that "heresy" in 435. Theodoret compiled a history of the church from A.D. 322 to A.D. 322 to A.D. 427.—*See Edw. Walford's Translation.*

Alexandria was ruled, for a short time, by Achillas.[1] He was succeeded by Alexander [in 312], who was the foremost in defending the doctrines of the gospel. Arius,[2] whose name was

---

[1] This bishop, who was supplanted by Alexander, is said to have been tinctured with the Meletian heresy.

[2] Arius (son of Ammonius), the celebrated originator of the Arian doctrines, was a presbyter of the Alexandrian Church, and presided over an independent parish of that city, by the name of Baucalis, where he had been placed a short time before Alexander became bishop. He was rigid ascetic, and acquired great respect from all. Socrates thus describes the advent of Arianism:— "After Peter of Alexandria had suffered martyrdom [A.D. 311], Achillas was installed in the episcopal office, whom Alexander succeeded. The latter bishop, in the fearless exercise of his functions for the instruction and government of the Church, attempted one day, in the presence of the presbytery and the rest of his clergy, to explain, with perhaps too philosophical minuteness, that great theological mystery,—the Unity of the Holy Trinity. A certain one of the presbyters under his jurisdiction, whose name was Arius, possessed of no inconsiderable logical acumen, imagining that the bishop entertained the same view of this subject as Sabellius the Libyan [African, who taught, in the third century, that there was but one person in the divine essence], controverted his statement with excessive pertinacity; advancing another error, which was directly opposed, indeed, to that which he supposed himself called upon to refute. 'If,' said he, 'the Father begat the Son, he that was begotten had a beginning of existence; and, from this, it is evident that there was a time when the Son was not in being. It, therefore, necessarily follows he had his existence from nothing.' Having drawn this inference from this novel train of reasoning, he excited many to a consideration of the question; and thus, from a little spark, a large fire was kindled."

Arius is thus described by the orthodox Epiphanius:— "He was exceedingly tall, with a clouded and serious brow, having the appearance of a man subdued by self-mortification. His dress corresponded with his look; his tunic was without sleeves, and his vest but half the usual length. His address was agreeable, and adapted to engage and fascinate all who heard him." He was a man of acknowledged learning, but not of the deepest philosophy.

Arius died suddenly at Constantinople, perhaps by the poison of his enemies, A.D. 336, and his opponents rejoiced at his death.—*See Dr. Murdock's note to Mosheim's Institutes, vol. I. p. 297, N.Y. edition, 1852.*

According to some historians, the idea of the Triad and Trinity originated with Plato, and was discussed by the Platonists.—*See Gibbon's Decline and Fall of Rome, chap. 21.*

then enrolled among the presbytery, and who was intrusted with the exposition of the Holy Scriptures, was induced to oppose Alexander's doctrines,—that the Son is equal with the Father, and of the same substance with God who begat him. Arius inveighed, in direct terms, against the truth, and affirmed that the Son of God is merely a creature, or created being, and that there was a time when he had no existence.

The other opinions which he advanced may be learned from his own writings.[1]

He taught these false doctrines, not only in the church, but also in general meetings and assemblies; and he even went from house to house, endeavoring to draw men over to his sentiments. Alexander, who was strongly attached to the doctrines of the Apostles, at first endeavored, by arguments and remonstrances, to convince him of his error; but when he found that he had had the madness to make a public declaration of his impiety, he ejected him from the order of the presbytery, according to the precept of the word of God,— "If thy right eye offend thee, pluck it out and cast it from thee."[2]

---

[1] The Orthodox and the Arians both believed Christ to be God, and so called him; but they differed on two points:—

1st, The Orthodox believed Christ's generation was *from eternity,* so that he was coeval with the Father; whereas the Arians believed he had a beginning.

2d, The Orthodox believed the Son to be derived of, and from, the Father, being of the same identical essence, and not merely of *similar* essence. But the Arians held that he was created by the power of God, out of nothing, although they allowed him to have been the first created being in the Universe.—*See the Letters of Arius and Alexander of Alexandria describing their own, and each other's conflicting opinions.*

[2] Socrates says that Alexander, the bishop of Alexandria, deposed Arius from his office and excluded him from the communion of the church, first at an assembly of the clergy in Alexandria, and then at a more numerous synod of Egyptian and Libyan bishops A.D. 321, composed of a hundred members. At this synod, however, the victory in the contest was *claimed* by both parties. Alexander published an epistle to his fellow ministers everywhere, notifying them of the excommunication of Arius, in which he makes use of the following language:— "Know, therefore, that there have recently arisen in our diocese, lawless and anti-Christian men, teaching apostasy such as one may justly consider and denominate the forerunner of Antichrist. I

CHAPTER IV.

INCREASE OF THE OPPOSITION TO ARIUS AND HIS HERESY.

At this time the Church of Rome was ruled by Silvester,[1] whose predecessor in the administration was Miltiades,[2] successor of Marcellinus. . . . . Alexander, who had become illustrious by his apostolic gifts, governed the church of Constantinople.

It was at this period, that Alexander, bishop of Alexandria, perceiving that many were deluded by the doctrines of Arius, communicated an account of his heresy, by letter, to the rulers of the principal churches. The following is the letter written by Alexander, bishop of Alexandria,[3] to his namesake, of Constantinople.

---

am constrained to warn you to pay no attention to the communications of Eusebius [of Nicomedia], should he write to you. . . . . . . The dogmas they assert, in utter contrariety to the Scriptures, and wholly of their own devising, are these:— That 'God was not always a Father; that the Word of God was not from eternity, but was made out of nothing; for that, the ever-existing God (the I Am, the eternal One) made him, who did not previously exist, out of nothing,'"

[1] This was the 12th year of Pope Silvester's "pontifical reign;" perhaps I should say, rather, "*bishoprick*," as the bishop of Alexandria was first called "pope," and the Roman pope did not acquire complete supremacy until it was conferred, by the tyrant Phocas, upon Boniface III., in the seventh century.—*See Baronius, A.D. 606*. This supremacy, some writers assert, was only a priority of rank.—*Bower's Lives of the Popes, vol. II.*

[2] Or Melchiades, as some call him.

[3] It was the custom, both at Alexandria and Rome, that all the churches should be under one bishop, but that each presbyter should have his own church, in which to assemble the people. So says Epiphanius, bishop of Salamis, in Cyprus, A.D. 367.—*See the edition of his writings by Dionysius Petavius.*

LETTER OF ALEXANDER, BISHOP OF ALEXANDRIA, TO ALEXANDER, BISHOP OF CONSTANTINOPLE, CONCERNING ARIUS AND THE ARIANS.

"Alexander sendeth greeting in the Lord to Alexander, the honored and beloved brother.

"Impelled by avarice and ambition, some evil-minded individuals have formed designs to obtain the highest ecclesiastical preferments. Under various pretexts, they trample upon the religion of the church; and being instigated by Satanic agency, they abandon all circumspection, and throw off the fear of God's judgments. Having been made to suffer by them in my own diocese, I write to arouse your caution, that you may be on your guard against them, lest they, or any of their party, should presume to enter your diocese. They are skillful in deception, and circulate false and specious letters, calculated to delude the simple and unwary.

"Arius and Achillas[1] have lately formed a conspiracy, and have acted even more culpably than Coluthus.[2] whom they rivalled in ambition. He reprehended their conduct, for he certainly had some pretext to plead in extenuation of his own guilt. When they perceived the gain resulting from his sale of ordinances, they felt unable to remain in subjection to the church; they accordingly constructed caverns, like those of robbers, in which they constantly assemble; and, day and night, they there invent calumnies against the Saviour, and against us. They revile the religious doctrines of the apostles; and, having, like the Jews, conspired against Christ, they deny his divinity, and declare him to be on a level with other men. They collect all those passages which allude to the incarnation of our Saviour, and to his having humbled himself for our salvation, and bring them forward as

---

[1] This is the same Achillas, or Achilles, who was some time ruler of the church at Alexandria, and who was succeeded by Alexander, the author of this epistle.

[2] Coluthus was one of the Alexandrian clergy, and seceded from Bishop Alexander's church about A.D. 319. He taught the heresy, that God is not the author of those just punishments which providentially afflict men. He ordained bishops without authority.—*Augustine on Heresies, Chap. 66.*

corroborative of their own impious assertion; while they evade all those which declare his divinity, and the glory which he possesses with the Father. They maintain the ungodly hypothesis entertained by the Greeks and the Jews, concerning Jesus Christ; and at the same time, endeavor, by every art, to ingratiate themselves with those people.

"All those suppositions connected with our religion, which have been advanced to excite derision, they represent as true. They daily excite persecutions and seditions against us. They bring accusations against us before judicial tribunals, suborning as witnesses certain unprincipled women, whom they have seduced into error. They dishonor Christianity by permitting young women to ramble about the streets.

"They have had the audacity to rend the seamless garment of Christ, which the people dared not divide. When their wicked course of life, which had been carefully concealed, became gradually known to us, we unanimously rejected them from the church which recognizes the divinity of Christ.

"They then ran hither and thither to form cabals against us, and endeavored, by means of fair words, to delude some among them into their own error. They are careful not to admit before them that they teach unholy doctrines and perpetrate infamous actions amongst us, and that they are for this cause excluded from communion with us.

"They conceal their pernicious doctrines by means of their plausible and persuasive mode of conversation; they thus deceive the unwary, while they never omit calumniating our religion on all occasions. Hence it arises that several have been led to sign their letters, and to receive them into communion. I consider that the conduct of our fellow ministers, in acting so rashly, is highly reprehensible; for they thus disobey the apostolic canons, and co-operate in the work of the devil against Christ. It is on this account that I make you acquainted, without delay, beloved brethren, with the unbelief of certain persons who say that there was a time when the Son of God had no existence; and that, not having existed from eternity, he must have had a beginning; and that when he was created, he was made like all other men that have ever been born. God, they say, created all things, and they include the Son of God in the number of creatures, both rational and irrational. To argue consistently, they, as a necessary consequence, affirm that he is by nature liable to change, and capable of both virtue and vice. Their hypothesis of his having been created, contradicts the testimony of the divine scriptures, which declare the immutability, the divinity, and the wisdom of the Word, which Word is Christ. 'We are also able,' say these evil-minded individuals, 'to become, like him, the sons of God,' for it is written, 'I have nourished and brought up children.' (Is. 1:2.) When the continuation of this text is brought before them, which is, 'and they have rebelled against me,' and it is objected that these words cannot refer to Christ, whose nature is immutable, they throw aside all reverence, and affirm that God foreknew and foresaw that his Son would not rebel against him, and that he therefore chose him in preference to all others. They likewise assert that he was not elected because he had by nature any qualifications superior to those of the other sons of God; for God, say they, has not any son by nature, nor, indeed, had he any connection whatever with him; they consider that he was elected because, though mutable by nature, he was vigilant and zealous in avoiding evil. They add that if Paul and Peter had made similar efforts, their filiation would in no respects have differed from his.

"To establish this absurd doctrine they pervert the Scriptures, and bring forward that expression in the Psalms, wherein is said of Christ, 'Thou hast loved righteousness and hated iniquity, therefore thy God hath anointed thee with the oil of gladness above thy fellows.' (Psalm xiv. 7.) That the Son of God was not created, and that there never was a time in which he did not exist, is expressly taught by John the Evangelist, who spoke of him as 'The only begotten Son which is in the bosom of the Father.' (John i. 18.) But he elsewhere affirms, that the Word of God is not to be classed among created beings; for he says, that 'all things were made by him,' and he also declares his individual existence in the following words: 'In the beginning was the Word, and the Word was with God, and the Word was God. All things were made by him, and without him, was not anything made that was made.' If, then, all things were made by him, how is it that He who bestowed existence on all, could at any period have had no existence himself? The Word who created cannot be of the same nature as the things created. For He was in the beginning, and all things were made by him, and were called by him out of nothing into being: he who is said to have existed before all things, must differ entirely form those things which were called out of nothing into being. This shows, likewise, that there is no separation between the Father and the Son, and that the idea of separation cannot even be conceived by the mind. The fact that the world was created out of nothing, shows that its creation is comparatively recent; for by the Father through the Son did all things which it contains receive their being. John, the pious apostle, perceiving the greatness of the Word of God above all created beings, could find no terms adequate to convey this truth, neither did he presume to apply the same epithet to the Maker as to the creature. The Son of God is not unbegotten, for the Father alone is unbegotten, but the manner in which the Son was begotten of God is inexplicable, and beyond the comprehension of the evangelist, and perhaps of angels. Therefore, I think that those should not be considered pious who presume to investigate this subject in disobedience to the injunction, 'Seek not what is too difficult for thee, neither inquire into what is too high for thee.' (Ecclus. iii. 21.) The knowledge of many things incomparably inferior is beyond the capacity of the human mind, and cannot therefore be attained.

"It has been said by Paul, 'Eye hath not seen, nor ear heard, neither have entered into the heart of man, the things which God hath prepared for them that love him.' (1 Cor. ii. 9.) God also said to Abraham, that 'the stars could not be numbered by him'; and it is likewise said, 'Who shall number the grains of sand by the sea-shore, or the drops of rain?' (Ecclus. i. 2.) How then can anyone, unless indeed his intellect be deranged, presume to inquire into the nature of the Word of God? It is said by the spirit of prophecy, 'Who shall declare his generation?' (Isa. liii. 8.) And, therefore, our Saviour said: 'No man knoweth the Son but the Father, and no man knoweth the Father save the Son.' (Matt. xi. 27.) It was, I think, concerning this same subject that the Father said, 'My secret is for me and for mine.' Paul has thus written concerning Christ, 'Whom he hath appointed heir of all things, by whom also he made the worlds.' (Heb. i. 2.) 'For by him were all things created that are in heaven, and that are in earth, visible and invisible, whether they be thrones, or dominions, or principalities, or powers, all things were created by him and for him, and he is before all things.' (Col. i. 16,17.) The Father is the Father because he has a Son, hence it is that he is called a Father. He did not beget his Son in time. Is it not impiety to say that the wisdom of God was at one period not in existence? for it is written, 'I was with Him, being joined to Him, I was his delight.' (Prov. viii.) The Sonship of our Saviour has nothing in common with the sonship of men. Wisdom is not susceptible of folly.

"Does not the apostle remark on this subject. 'What communion hath light with darkness? and what concord hath Christ with Belial?' (2 Cor. vi. 14, 15), and Solomon said that he could not comprehend 'the way of a serpent upon a rock' (Prov. xxx. 19), which, according to St. Paul, is Christ. And it is, on this account, that our Lord, being, by nature, the Son of the Father, is worshipped by all. Paul says God spared not his own Son, but delivered him up for us, who are not by nature his sons. (Rom. viii. 32.) It is also written, 'This is my beloved son (Matt. iii. 17); and in the Psalms, it is written that the Saviour said, 'The lord said unto me, Thou art my Son.' (Ps. ii. 7.) But what can these words signify, 'I conceived thee in my bosom before the star of morn,' unless they are meant to show that he was born according to the course of nature of the Father? But there are others not his children by nature, as it is written in the word, 'The sons of God saw the daughters of men, and took them as wives.' (Gen. vi. 2.) And God, speaking by Isaiah, said, 'I have begotten and brought up children, and they rebelled against me.' (Isa. i. 2.)

"Three bishops in Syria [Eusebius, of Cæsarea; Theodotus, of Laodicea; and Paulinus, of Tyre], ordained, no one knows how, side with them, and incite them to plunge deeper and deeper into iniquity.

"They reject those passages of Scripture which declare in our Saviour's glory and union with the Father. Such as: 'My

Father and I are one.' 'Lord, show us the Father.' In reply to which he said, 'He that hath seen me hath seen the Father. And in the Psalms, 'In the light we shall see light. (Ps. xxxv.)

"They say that they alone are wise and destitute of property. Oh, what wicked arrogance! Even devils are not guilty of impiety like this. These ignorant persons contend that one of the two things must necessarily be true; either that Christ was created, or that there are two unbegotten beings.

"We believe, as is taught by the apostolical church, in the only unbegotten Father, who is the author of his own existence. The mind of man could not possibly invent a term expressive of what is meant by being unbegotten. To say that the Son was, that he has always been, and that he existed before all ages, is not to say that he is unbegotten. We believe that he is the only begotten Son of God, as was taught by the holy men who vainly endeavored to clear up the mystery, but failed, and confessed that it was beyond their powers.

"Besides this pious opinion of the Father and the Son, we confess the existence of the Holy Ghost, which truth has been upheld by the saints of the Old Testament, and by the learned divines of the New.

"We believe in one catholic and apostolical church, which cannot be destroyed, and which never fails to defeat all the impious designs of heretics. Besides this we receive the doctrine of the resurrection from the dead, of which Jesus Christ, our Lord, became the first fruits. He possessed a true, not a suppositious body, and he derived it from Mary, the mother of God.[1]

" I have sent you these signatures by my son Apion, the deacon : they are the signatures of the ministers in all Egypt and in Thebes ; also of those in Libya. Pentapolis, Syria, Lycia, Pamphylia, Asia, Cappadocia, and in the other adjoining countries. You likewise must follow this example. Many attempts have been made by me to gain back those who have been led astray, and discover the means of restoring the people who have been deceived by them; and I found none more persuasive in leading them to repentance, than the manifestation of the union

---

[1] Epiphanius says (*Haeres,* 69, 4) that Alexander sent seventy copies of this letter into the different provinces.

of our fellow ministers. The following are the name of those who have been excommunicated:—

" Among the presbyters, Arius; among the deacons, Achillas, Euzoius, Aithalis,[1] Lucius, Sarmatis, Julius,[2] Menas, another Arius, and Helladius." Alexander wrote in the same strain to Philogonius, bishop of Antioch; to Eustathius, who than ruled the Church of the Bereans, and to others.

But Arius could not quietly acquiesce in this. He, therefore, wrote to all those who he thought were of his sentiments.[3] The following is his letter to Eusebius, bishop of Nicomedia.

---

[1] These names are of various orthography, Socrates writing Aithales, and Sozomen Aithalas. The latter spells the eighth name Minas, but he is considered a little less reliable than Socrates. As I shall have occasion to quote often from his [Sozomen's] ecclesiastical history, it seems proper to give a sketch of him in this place.

Hermias Sozomen Salamanes, according to the very learned Valesius, who wrote his life, was born and educated in Palestine, probably at Gaza, in the bosom of those monks who were of his relative, Alaphio's family; and he studied the civil law at Berytus, a city of Phœnicia, where was a famous law-school. His ancestors were of Bethelia, near Gaza, where his grandfather was born and converted to Christianity. Sozomen practiced law at Constantinople at the same time with Socrates Scholasticus; and as they each wrote a history of the same events, it is evident one purloined from the other without giving due credit. Socrates probably wrote first. So Valesius thinks. Sozomen's Church history extends from A.D. 324 to 440. His style is more perspicuous and consecutive than that of Socrates.—*See Bohn's edition of their works, in English.*

[2] Socrates calls them Samartes and Julian; and the names of Carpones and Gaius are given in Alexander's letter to his fellow ministers, as among these apostates.

[3] This is the statement of Theodoret, and the letter of Arius which follows, is his copy of that document, as also the epistle of Eusebius of Nicomedia to Paulinus of Tyre.

CHAPTER V.

LETTER OF ARIUS TO HIS FRIEND, EUSEBIUS OF NICOMEDIA. DESCRIBING
HIS DOCTRINES, WHICH OCCASION THE OPPOSITION AND SEVERITIES
OF ALEXANDER; AND LETTER OF EUSEBIUS OF NOCIMEDIA, TO
PAULINUS OF TYRE, ON THE SAME SUBJECT, ETC.;

LETTER OF ARIUS TO EUSEBIUS.

"Arius, unjustly persecuted by the Pope Alexander, on account of that all-conquering truth, which you also uphold,
sendeth greeting in the Lord to his very dear lord, the man of
God, the faithful and orthodox Eusebius.

"Ammonius, my father, being about to depart for
Nicomedia, I consider myself bound to salute you by him, and
withal to address myself to that natural affection which you bear
towards the brethren, for the sake of God and of Christ; appris-
ing you that the bishop oppresses and persecutes us most
severely, and that he causes us much suffering. He has driven us
out of the city as atheists, because we do not concur in what he
publicly preaches; namely, that the Father has always been, and
that the Son has always been. That as the Father, so is the Son;
that the Son is unbegotten as the Father; that he is always being
begotten, without having been begotten; that neither by thought,
nor by any interval, does God precede the Son, God and the Son
having always been; and that the Son proceeds from God.

"Eusebius, your brother bishop of Cæsarea, Theodotius,
Paulinus, Athanasius [of Anazarbus], Gregory, Ætius, and all
the bishops of the East, have been condemned because they say
that God had an existence, prior to that of the Son, except
Philogonius Hellanicus, and Macarius, who are unlearned men,
and who have embraced heretical opinions. One of them says
that the Son is an effusion, another that he is an emission, the
other that he is also unbegotten. These are impieties to which we
could not listen, even though the heretics should threaten us with

a thousand deaths.[1] But we say and believe, and have taught, and do teach, that the Son is not unbegotten, nor in any way unbegotten, even in part; and that he does not derive his subsistence from any matter; but that, by his will and counsel, he has subsisted before time, and before ages, as perfect God; only begotten and unchangeable; and that he existed not before he was begotten, or created, or purposed, or established; for he was not begotten. We are persecuted because we say that the Son had a beginning, but that God was without beginning. This is really the cause of our persecution; and, likewise, because we say he is from nothing [from not anything]. And this we say, because he

---

[1] Arius intended, by no means, to lower the dignity of Christ by ascribing to him a beginning of existence. He would ascribe to him the greatest dignity which a being could have after God, without entirely ignoring the distinction between that being and God. Still he did not hesitate to ascribe to him the name of God. Probably he appealed to those passages of scripture where the name of God seems to be applied, in an improper sense, to created beings, and thence argued that it was also applied in an analogous manner, but in the highest sense, to the Logos.—*Neander Ch. Hist.,* ii 362-4.

Gibbon says the most implacable enemies of Arius have acknowledged the learning and blameless life of that eminent presbyter, who, in a former election, had perhaps declined the proffered episcopal throne in favor of Alexander of Alexandria, his subsequent first great opponent in Egypt. This last statement is one the authority of Philostorgius, the Arian.—*See Decline and Fall,* II. *chap.* 21.

Philostorgius says [book I. chap 3] that "when the people, by their votes, were on the point of electing Arius, he declined the honor in favor of Alexander," who, soon after his election, got involved in doctrinal disputes with the same friend, and never rested till the former had been twice excommunicated, and, at last, banished by an imperial edict, and anathematized by the universal Synod of Nice. This Philostorgius, the heretic and apologist of Arius, was a native of Cappadocia, born A.D. 364, of humble parentage. Coming to Constantinople to complete his studies, he there remained, and became either a lawyer or an ecclesiastic. He wrote a history of the church, in twelve books, beginning with the schism of Arius, and extending to A.D. 425. The work, as he compiled it, is lost; but a brief epitome of it is preserved by the Orthodox Photius, a noted patriarch of Constantinople, A.D. 853. Of course the original text was Greek, like that of all the early ecclesiastical histories in that part of the Roman Empire.—*See Bohn's edition. translated for the first time in English by Edw. Walford.*

is neither part of God, nor of any subjacent matter. For this are we persecuted; the rest you know. Farewell."

Of those whose names are mentioned in this letter, Eusebius was bishop of Cæsarea, Theodotius was bishop of Laodicea, Paulinus of Tyre, Ætius of Lydda, which is now called Diospolis. Philogonius was bishop of Antioch, Hellanicus of Tripolis, and Macarius of Jerusalem.

When Eusebius of Nicomedia received the epistle, he wrote as follows to Paulinus, bishop of Tyre.

LETTER OF EUSEBIUS TO PAULINUS

To my Lord Paulinus, Eusebius sendeth greeting in the Lord.

"The zeal of my Lord Paulinus, and likewise his silence concerning the truth, have not failed to reach our ears, If, on the one hand, we have rejoiced on account of the zeal of my lord, on the other, we have grieved, because the silence of such a man appears like the condemnation of our cause.

"Hence, as it behooves not a wise man to be of a different opinion from others, and yet to be silent concerning the truth, I exhort you to stir up within yourself the spirit of wisdom, that you may be able to write what may be profitable to yourself and to others; which will certainly be the case, if you will examine the Holy Scriptures, and follow them in your writings. We have never heard that there are two unbegotten beings, nor that one has been divided into two. We have neither been taught, my Lord, nor do we believe that the Divinity has ever undergone any change of a temporal nature; but we affirm that there is one who is unbegotten, and that there also exists another who did in truth proceed from him, yet who was not made out of his substance, and who does not at all participate in the nature or substance of him who is unbegotten. We believe him to be entirely distinct in nature and in power, and yet to be a perfect likeness, in character and in power, of him from whom he originated.

"We believe that the mode of his beginning cannot be expressed by any words; and that it is incomprehensible, not only to man, but also to orders of beings superior to man. These opinions we advance, not as having derived them from our own imagination, but as having deduced them from Scripture; whence we learn that the Son was created, established, and begotten in the same substance, and in the same immutable and inexpressible nature as the Maker; and so the Lord says, 'God created me in the beginning of His way; I was set up from everlasting; before the hills was I brought forth;' (Prov. viii. 22-26.) If he had preceded from Him or of Him, as a portion of Him, or by an efflux of His substance, it could not be said that he was created or established; and of this you, my lord, are certainly not ignorant. For that which proceeds from Him who is unbegotten, cannot be said to have been created or founded, either by Him or by another since He has been begotten, from the beginning. . .

"There is, indeed, nothing which partakes of His substance; yet, every thing which exists, has been called into being by His will, for He verily is God. All things were made in his likeness, and in the future likeness of His Son, being created according to His will. All things were made by the Son, and through God. All things are of God.

"When you have received my letter, and have revised it according to the knowledge and grace given you by God, I beg you will write, as soon as possible, to my Lord Alexander. I feel confident that if you will write to him, you will succeed in bringing him over to your opinion."[1]

"When blasphemous doctrines," says Theodoret, "became disseminated in the churches of Egypt and of the East, disputes and contentions arose in every city, and in every village, con-

---

[1] Eusebius, of Cæsarea, wrote a letter to the bishop Alexander, in which he sought to convince him that he was doing Arius injustice; and that, if he would but rightly conceive him, he would find no difficulty in coming to an agreement with him. A fragment of this letter has been preserved, and is to be found in the 6th act of the Second Nicene Council.—*Neander's Hist. Ch. Relg. and Chch.* II 369, *Torrey's 3d American edition.*

The second Council of Nice was held A.D. 787, in the time of Leo the Great, Pope of Rome. The most noted dogma established at this second Synod of Nice, was that in favor of paying respect, and even *adoration* (which some call "*worship*"), to certain images and symbols of divine things.

cerning theological dogmas. The common people, being witnesses of these controversies, took part,—some with one party
and some with the other. Those who had been most friendly
hitherto, now fought against each other with their tongues
instead of spears."[1]

---

[1] Coluthus, mentioned on page 38, *ante,* was one of the contentious
presbyters in Egypt, who teaching the heretical doctrine, that God was
not the creator of the wicked nor of wickedness and evil in any sense,
although a bitter opponent of Arius, was called to account by a Council
held in Alexandria, A.D. 324. He had assumed the authority of a bishop.
His heresy was condemned and himself deposed.

CHAPTER VI.

THE GENERAL COUNCIL OF NICE—THE EMPEROR CONVOKES THE BISHOPS FROM ALL CHRISTENDOM.

The Emperor Constantine, who possessed the most profound wisdom, had no sooner heard of the troubles of the
church, than he endeavored to put a stop to them.
He, therefore dispatched a messenger of considerable
sagacity [Hosius, bishop of Cordova] to Alexandria with letters,
hoping thereby to reconcile the disputants.[1] But, not succeeding,

---

[1]   Socrates is more explicit on this head. He says, "When the
emperor was made acquainted with these disorders, he was very deeply
grieved. . . . . . He sent a letter to Alexander and Arius, by a trustworthy
person named Hosius, who was bishop of Cordova, in Spain, and whom
the emperor loved and held in the highest estimation." The letter began
thus: "Victor Constantine Maximus Augustus to Alexander and Arius.
Your present controversy, I am informed, originated thus: When you,
Alexander, inquired of your presbyters what were the sentiments of each
on a certain inexplicable passage of the *written Word,* thereby mooring
a subject improper for discussion, you, Arius, rashly gave expression to
a view of the matter, such as ought, either never to have been
conceived, or if, indeed, it had been suggested to your mind, it became
you to bury in silence.

.   .   .   .

For, indeed, how few are capable either of adequately expounding, or
even accurately understanding the import of matters so vast and
profound!   Who can grapple with the subtilties of such investigations,
without danger of lapsing into excessive error?   Let there be one faith,
one sentiment, and one covenant of the Godhead.

But respecting those minute investigations, which ye enter into
among yourselves with so much nicety, even if ye should not concur in
one judgment, it becomes you to confine them to your own reflections,
and to keep them in the secret recesses of the mind. . . . . . . Resume the
exercise of mutual friendship and grace."

However, neither Alexander nor Arius was softened by this appeal;
and, moreover, there was incessant strife and tumult among the people.
But another source of disquietude had pre-existed there, which served to

he proceeded to summon the celebrated Council of Nice;[1] and commanded that the bishops, and those connected with them, should be mounted on the asses, mules, and horses belonging to the public, in order to repair thither. When all those who were capable of enduring the fatigue of the journey, had arrived at Nice, he went thither himself, as much from the wish of seeing the bishops, as from the desire of preserving unanimity amongst them. He arranged that all their wants should be liberally supplied. Three hundred and eighteen bishops were assembled. The bishop of Rome, on account of his very advanced age, was necessarily absent; but he sent two presbyters[2] to the Council, for the purpose of taking part in all the transactions. At this period, individuals were richly endowed with apostolical gifts; and many, like the holy apostles, bore in their bodies the marks of the Lord Jesus Christ.[3]

James, bishop of Antioch, a city of Mygdonia, which is called Nisbis by the Syrians and Assyrians, had power to raise the dead, and to restore them to life; he performed many won-

---

trouble the churches, though it was confined to the eastern parts. This arose from some desiring to keep the Feast of the Passover, or Easter, more in accordance with the customs of the Jews, while others preferred the mode of celebration used by the Christians in general throughout the world. These were the causes which led Constantine to convoke the Council of Nice.

[1] Nice anciently called Nicæa, was a city of Bithynia. It is now called Izneek, or Iznik, and is a village and ruined city on the eastern extremity of Lake Izneek, in Asia Minor, between Ismead and Brusa. It was the first conquest of the Crusaders in the East, A.D. 1097.

[2] Vito and Vincentius were their names, says Sozomen and other historians.

[3] Of the *ten persecutions*, the first was that of Nero, A.D. 64; the second, of Domitian, A.D. 95; the third, of Trajan, 107; the fourth, Adrian, 118; the fifth, of Caracalla, 212; the sixth, of Maximin, 235; the seventh, of Decius, 250; the eighth, of Valerian, 257; the ninth, of Aurelian, 274; and the tenth, and most severe, was begun on Christmas Days, A.D. 303, under Diocletian, when the emperor ordered the doors of the Christian church of Nicomedia to be barred, and then burnt the edifice with every soul within, the number being six hundred. Nicomedia, the chief city of Bithynia, was then the seat of the imperial court, Constantinople not being made such until A.D. 328.

derful miracles. Paul, bishop of Neo-Cæsarea, a fortress situated on the banks of the Euphrates, had suffered much from the cruelty of Licinius. He had been deprived of the use of both hands by the application of a red-hot iron, by which the nerves which give motion to the muscles had been contracted and destroyed. Some had the right eye torn out; others had lost the right arm. Among the latter sufferers was Paphnutius,[1] of Egypt. In short, this was an assembly of martyrs. Yet this holy and celebrated assembly was not free from those of a contentious spirit; there were certainly few of this class, yet they were as dangerous as sunken rocks, for they concealed the evil, while they profanely coincided in the blasphemy of Arius.

---

[1] According to other authors, he had suffered his right *eye* to be cut out. Perhaps the word "latter" refers to only part of the last clause, not to that respecting his arm.

CHAPTER VII.

THE COUNTRIES WHICH WERE REPRESENTED AT THE UNIVERSAL
SYNOD.—INTERESTING CHARACTERS, CONFESSORS, ETC.,
PRESENT.—PRELIMINARY DISPUTATIONS.—THREE DISTINCT
PARTIES.—ARIUS SUMMONED.—ATHANASIUS APPEARS.

Those who held the chief places among the ministers of God
were convened from all the churches which have filled all
Europe, Africa, and Asia.[1] And one sacred edifice, dilated, as it
were, by God, contained within it, on the same occasion, both
Syrians and Cilicians, Phœnicians, Arabs and Palestinians, and
in addition to these, Egyptians, Thebans, Libyans, and those
who came from Mesopotamia.[2]   And, at this Synod, a bishop

---

[1]   I take these sketches from Socrates, where he transcribes
Eusebius Pamphilus but partly from "*De Vita Constantini*" itself: Liber
III ch. 7.   Mansi (II 1073) says there were probably 2,000 persons
attending the Council.
[2]   A complete list of the bishops present is not in existence,
although Socrates says there was such a list in he *Synodicon* of
Athanasius, a book which is not known to be now extant.
    The following are all the names I can gather from the ancient
records.   The greatest number were Orientals.   Those of known Arian
proclivities are designated by stars (*).   They may be considered the
leading men of that party in the Nicene Synod.

    ACESIUS, Novatian bishop of Constantinople.
    ÆTIUS, * of Lydda in Syria.
    ALEXANDER, of Alexandria in Egypt; the first orthodox opponent of
Arius.
    ALEXANDER, of Byzantium, the correspondent of Alexander, of
Alexandria.
    AMPHION, of Epiphania in Cilicia.
    AMPHION, * of Sidon.
    ANTHONY, * of Tarsus in Cilicia, who subsequently became a
bishop.
    ARIUS, of Alexandria in Egypt; the originator of Arianism, who was
anathematized by the Council, and banished by the emperor.
    AROSTANES alias ARISTENS, or ARISTACES, who converted the king
of Greater Armenia to Christianity.

ATHANASIUS, * of Anazarbus in Cilicia.

ATHANASIUS, of Alexandria in Egypt; the great future defender of the Nicene Creed, though he was only a deacon of the Council.

AUXANON, a boy (attendant of Acesius, the Novatian), who lived to a great age, and was presbyter of the Novatians. He wrote many curious details of the Council.—*Stanley. Neale.*

BASIL, * of Amasia in Pontus.

CAPITO, of Sicily.

CÆCILLIAN, of Carthage in Africa.

CYNON.

DACHIUS, * of Berenice.

DOMNUS, of Stridon in Pannonia.

EULALIUS, * of Cappadocia.

EUPSYCHIUS, of Tyana, in Cappadocia.

EUSEBIUS, * of Nicomedia, the chief town of Bithynia; he was the great friend and defender of Arius; Constantine was baptized by him.

EUSEBIUS PAMPHILUS, * of Cæsarea in Palestine, whom Gibbon calls "the most learned of the theologians." Dean Stanley calls him the clerk of the Imperial closet, chaplain, interpreter, &c.

EUSTATHIUS, of Antioch in Syria; one of the chief debaters of the Orthodox party; and. according to Theodoret, the one who delivered the opening oration before the emperor.

EUSTORGIUS, from Milan.

EUTYCHIUS, of Amasena; successor to Basil, the martyr.

GREGORY, * of Berytus is Syria.

HARPOCRATION, of Cuonopolis in Egypt.

HELLANNICUS, of Tripolis.

HERMOGENES, the deacon, Secretary of the Council; afterwards bishop of Cæsarea.

HOSIUS, of Cordova, in Spain; chief counsellor, in ecclesiastical affairs in the West, to Constantine; of whom Athanasius writes, "Was not he, old Hosius, presiding over the Synod?"—*Apol. de Fuga*, II 5.

HYPATIUS, of Gangra in Pamphilia, who suffered martyrdom, being stoned by the Novatians.

JAMES, of Antioch, alias Nisbis, in Mygdonia, who was reputed to be able to perform miracles, and to raise the dead.

JOHN, the Persian.

LEONTIUS, subsequently bishop of Cæsarea in Cappadocia, who was called a prophet.

LONGINUS, of Neo-Cæsarea in Pontus.

LONGINUS, * of Cappadocia.

MACARIUS, of Jerusalem, whom Athanasius classes among the most distinguished opponents of Arianism.

MARCELLUS, bishop of Ancyra in Galatia, a person of weight in the Council.

MARCUS, of Calabria.

MARIS, * of Chalcedon in Bithynia, who was banished by the emperor for Arianism soon after the Nicene Council.

MELETIUS, * of Thebes.

MELETIUS, * of Sebastopolis in Pontus.

MENOPHANTES, * of Ephesus in Ionia.

NARCISSUS, * of Neronopolis in Cilicia.

NICASIUS, of Dijon, France.

NICHOLAS, of Myra in Lycia, the same as our Santa Claus. This bishop was not one of those who signed the Decrees, and it is doubtful if he was present. But many legends connect him with this great Council of Nicæa.

PAPHNUTIUS, of Upper, Thebes, which is now Upper Egypt. He had lost his right eye and both his legs in the Maximinian persecution. He was a reputed worker of miracles.

PATROPHILUS, * of Scythopolis in Galilee.

PAULINUS, * of Tyre in Phœnicia.

PAUL, Secretary of Alexander of Byzantium, 12 years old.

PAULUS, or PAUL, of Neo-Cæsarea, upon Euphrates. He had had his hands withered by hot irons, and been horribly tortured otherwise in the persecutions, by order of Licinius.

PISTUS, of Athens in Attica.

POTAMON, of Heraclea in Egypt, who had lost an eye in the Maximinian persecution.

PROTOGENES of Sardica in Thrace.

SECUNDUS, * of Theuchira.

SECUNDUS, * of Ptolemais in Egypt, who was one of the two Arians excommunicated.

SENTIANUS, of Boreum.

SPYRIDON, or SPIRIDION, of Trimithus in Cyprus, the shepherd-bishop who had lost his right eye in the persecution of Maximin. He was said to be a miracle worker.

TARCODINATUS, * of Ægæ.

THEODORET, * bishop of Heraclea in Thrace.

THEODOTIUS, * of Laodicea, who is sometimes called THEODORUS.

THEOGNIS, * of Nice in Bithynia, where the Council was held, who was also soon banished for Arianism.

THEOPHILUS, bishop of the Goths on the Danube, teacher of Ulfilas.

ZOPHYRUS, * of Barca.

THEONAS, * of Marmarica in Africa, now called Barca.

THEOPHILUS, bishop of the Goths on the Danube.

from Persia was also among them; neither was the Scythian absent from this assemblage. Pontus also, and Galatia, Pamphylia, Cappadocia, Asia, and Phrygia, supplied those, who were most distinguished among them. Besides, there met there Thracians and Macedonians, Achaians and Epirots, and even those who dwelt still more distant that these. The most celebrated among the Spaniards[1] took his seat among the rest. The prelate of the

---

TRYPHILLIUS.

VINCENT or VINCENTIUS, of Rome, one of the pope's legates, a presbyter, as was also

VITO, alias VICTOR, another legate of Silvester, the Roman pope, who was too aged to attend in person. This was his twelfth papal year.

Most of the bishops were Greeks. The Latins were Hosius, Cecilian of Carthage, Marcus of Calabria, Nicasius of Dijon, Domnus of Stridon, Victor and Vincent.

As to the exact number of bishops at the Council, the best authorities differ considerably. In another place (book I chap. 11), Theodoret, quoting from Eustathius, states it as 270. Athanasius makes the number 318 in two places in his writings, which is the number given by Jerome in his *Chronicon*. Epiphanius, likewise, twice gives the same number. Hilary and Rufinus give the same. Sozomen says there were "about 320." Marius Victorinus, who lived nearly at the same time, states the number to have been 315. Socrates calls it 300 in his copy of Eusebius Pamphilus' account, although the latter, himself, sets it at only 250. Valesius says, that in the Greek collection of the canons of Nice, the notation of the time is prefixed thus:— "The canons of the 318 holy fathers, convened at Nice, in the consulate of the most illustrious Paulinus and Julianus, on the 636th year from Alexander, on the 19th day of the month Desius, before the 13th of the Kalends of July." The number of bishops probably varied at different periods of the Council, some arriving and others leaving.

[1] This was Hosius, bishop of Cordova. Gibbon thinks he presided over the Nicene Council. He probably founds his opinion upon the words of Athanasius, in *"The Apology for his Flight,"* one of the numerous works of Athanasius. The passage is thus: "Over that Synod was not old Hosius, himself, presiding?" [book II chap. 5]. There were several who are said to have presided. Pope Hadrian, in some of his writings, represents the two legates of Silvester as presiding with Hosius. These were Vito, whom we called Victor, and Vincentius.—*See Baronius*, IV. 93.

imperial city [Constantinople] was absent through age; but his presbyters were present, and filled his place.

Such a crown, composed as a bond of peace, the Emperor Constantine alone has ever dedicated to Christ his Saviour, as a thank-offering to God for victory over his enemies, having appointed this convocation among us in imitation of the apostolical assembly.[1] For, among them, it is said, were convened "devout men of every nation under heaven." That congregation, however, was inferior in this respect, that all present were not ministers of God; whereas, in this assembly, the number of bishops exceeded two hundred and fifty. The number of the presbyters, deacons, and acolyths (or young priests), who attended them, was almost incalculable. Some of these ministers of God were eminent for their wisdom; some for the strictness of their life and patient endurance of persecution; and others united in themselves all these distinguished characteristics. Some were venerable from their advanced age; others were conspicuous for their youth and vigor of mind; and others had but recently entered on their ministerial career. For all these, the emperor had appointed an abundant supply of daily food to be provided."

Socrates, who quotes most of the foregoing report of Eusebius Pamphilus, continues the description thus:—

"There were, among the bishops, two of extraordinary celebrity—Paphnutius, bishop of Upper Thebes, and Spyridon, bishop of Cyprus. The *former* was reputed to possess power to perform miracles. He had lost his right eye in time of persecution, through his adherence to the Christian faith. The emperor honored him exceedingly, and often kissed the part where the eye had been torn out. The *latter* was a shepherd, and continued to feed his sheep during his prelacy. He was reputed to have miraculous power, and even to be able to raise the dead and restore them to life.

Many of the laity were also present, who were practised in the art of reasoning, and each prepared to advocate the cause of his own party .[2] Eusebius, bishop of Nicomedia,[3] supported the

---

[1] See Acts II 5.

[2] There seems to have been three distinct parties at this Council— first, the strictly *Arian*; secondly, the radical *Orthodox*, and thirdly, the

opinion of Arius, together with Theognis, bishop of Nice, and Maris, bishop of Chalcedon, in Bithynia. These were powerfully opposed by Athanasius,[1] a deacon of the Alexandrian Church, who was highly esteemed by Alexander, his bishop, and on the account was much envied.

---

conservative, who occupied a middle ground between the two principal parties. It was the Orthodox party that introduced the word "consubstantial" to describe the oneness of Christ and God, which prevailed and has ever been retained among the great Christian-Church doctrines. Some of the chief Arians were Eusebius, of Nicomedia, and Theognis (both personal friends to Arius, himself), Secundus and Theonas. Some of the leading Orthodox were Hosius, Eustathius, Alexander, and Athanasius. The first of the conservatives was Eusebius, of Cæsarea, that is, Pamphilus, the historian, who originated what has been called semi-Arianism. This distinguished man—born at Cæsarea, in Palestine, A.D. 270—was surnamed for his ever intimate friend and companion, Pamphylus, or Pamphilus, the martyr of Cæsarea, whose extensive library became the source whence Eusebius drew deep draughts of learning. After the martyrdom of his friend, in 309, he fled, first to Tyre and thence to Egypt, where he resided till the persecution subsided. On returning to Cæsarea, about 314, he was ordained bishop of his native city. He died about A.D. 340. His works are very numerous, but many of them are now lost. Among those extant, the more important are his *"Chronicon," "Ecclesiastical History," "Apology for Origen," "Life of Constantine the Great," "Evangelical Preparation,"* &c.

[3] See his letter to Paulinus, bishop of Tyre. This was the Eusebius from whom the Arians had the name of "Eusebians." In one of Constantine's letters to the people of Nicomedia, quoted by Theodoret in his Ecclesiastical History, this Eusebius is charged by the emperor with hostile behavior, and with favoring Maxentius, the tyrant, a short time prior to the Nicene Council. Nevertheless, he subsequently became so intimate with the emperor, that his influence helped to bring the Arians into political favor. It was this bishop who baptized Constantine. He was sometimes called "Eusebius the Great" by his partisans. Next to Arius, he shared the bitterest resentment of the Orthodox in his day.

[1] Athanasius, in less than a year, succeeded Alexander, and became bishop of Alexandria, which office he held over forty years. Alexander died in five months after the Council of Nice. Gibbon calls Athanasius the most sagacious of the theologians of his time. He became the greatest champion of his party against the Arians.

For a short time previous to the general assembling of the bishops, the disputants engaged in preparatory logical contests with various opponents; and, when many were attracted by the interest of their discourse, one of the laity, who was a man of unsophisticated understanding, and had stood the test of persecution, reproved these reasoners, telling them that Christ and his apostles did not teach us the dialectic art, nor vain subtleties, but simple-mindedness, which is preserved by faith and good works.

ANOTHER ACCOUNT OF THE SAME TRANSACTIONS, WITH SOME ADDITIONAL CIRCUMSTANCES.

Before the appointed day on which the discussion of the questions which had brought them together had arrived, the bishops assembled together,[1] and, having summoned Arius to attend, began to examine the disputed topics, each one among them advancing his own opinion, and many different questions started out of the investigation. Some of the bishops spoke against the introduction of novelties contrary to the faith which had been delivered to them from the beginning, and some agreed that the faith of God ought to be received without curious inquiries. Others, however, contended that former opinions ought not to be retained without examination. Many of the bishops and of the inferior clergy attracted the notice of the emperor and the court by these disputations, and Athanasius, in particular, greatly distinguished himself on the preliminary assemblies.

Hermias here proceeds to narrate the miracle, as he calls it, by which a heathen philosopher was confounded and converted by a simple old man, who advised him not to expend his labor in vain by striving to disprove facts which could only be understood by *faith*. The hero of this exploit is said to have been Spyridon, the shepherd-bishop. "Certain of the pagan philosophers," it is asserted by our author, "were desirous of taking part in the discussions—some to get information as to the doctrine that was inculcated, and others to stigmatize them with en-

---

[1] This account I quote from Hermias Sozomen.

gaging in a strife about words. . . The bishops held long consultations; and, after summoning Arius before them, inquired diligently into his doctrines, yet, at the same time, withholding their final decision."

CHAPTER VIII.

MEETING OF THE COUNCIL IN THE IMPERIAL PALACE. —PRESENCE OF
CONSTANTINE.—HIS SPLENDID APPEARANCES AND SPEECHES.

Another day appointed for the Council, and upon which the
disputes were to be terminated,[1] when every one of whom the
Synod consisted would, of course, be in attendance, a large
number of seats were placed in the middle hall, itself, of the
palace, this apartment being apparently more spacious than any
other. The seats having been arranged in a row on either side, all
who had been summoned coming in, sat down together, each in
his own place. Then the whole Council, with dignified, modesty,
becoming calm, all for the first time preserved silence, awaiting
the approach of the emperor. Presently one of his most intimate
friends entered, then another and another. He himself was pre-

---

[1]   This is the account given by Eusebius Pamphilus, bishop of
Cæsarea, in his life of Constantine, from which I translate.   Eusebius,
being an eye-witness of what he describes, as well as "the most learned
of the Christian prelates," as Gibbon declares, his report is worthy of
credit and high regard.—*See Life of Con., book* III. *chaps.* 10-16,
inclusive.
       Some critical remarks of Socrates are worthy of notice here.   That
historian says,— "Eusebius, surnamed Pamphilus, has composed a
history of the church in ten books, brought down to the time of the
Emperor Constantine, when the persecution ceased which Diocletian
had commenced against the Christians [A.D. 309].   But, in writing the
life of Constantine, this author has very slightly treated of the Arian
controversy, being evidently more intent on a highly wrought eulogium
of the emperor, than an accurate statement of facts."   Eusebius gives no
description of the Nicene Council in his ecclesiastical history.
       Nevertheless, I consider Eusebius more *accurate* and *consientious*
than Socrates.   Eusebius seems to have had a feeble judgment in respect
to human character.   His ability to judge of *divine* character, as he
plainly acknowledges, was inferior to that of the hardy old soldier,
Constantine.

ceded not by soldiers and a number of guards, according to the common custom, but by some of his friends only, who professed the faith of Christ. A certain signal, by which the arrival of the emperor was to be announced, being given, that all might rise, at last he came advancing along midway, as if some celestial messenger of God, by the glittering of the purple robe verily dazzling the eyes of all, and flaming, as it were, gleaming in the sunbeams, being adorned by the utmost splendor of gold and precious stones.

And the elegance of his person was, indeed, equally conspicuous.

As he has true regard for the soul, it appeared natural that he should be adorned with the fear of God and with religion. And this his downcast eyes, the flush upon his countenance, and the motion of his body, as well as his step, all indicated. But, as the other appearance of his person, so, also, his height evidently surpassed that of all who were around him. And yet, his stature was not the only superior excellence of his aspect, for the symmetry of his form, and its elegance, so to speak,—the majestic mien, and, finally, the robustness, being unequaled. To which personal superiority, truly wonderful in itself, all modesty being added, tempered, as it was, by imperial lenity, proclaimed the excellence of his mind worthy of, and even above, all praise.

The emperor, coming to the head of the seats, at first stood. And a low chair, made of gold, was placed before him; but he did not incline to sit down till the bishops nodded assent to him.[1] After the emperor, all the rest seated themselves. Then that bishop, who occupied the first seat on the emperor's right,[2]

---

[1] Sozomen says the emperor motioned to the members to be seated, after seating himself. He says, also, the palace was a large and beautiful edifice.

[2] It would seem probable, that he, who is here referred to, was the first in authority at the Council, after the emperor. If it was not the writer, himself, why does he withhold the name of so prominent a man? Theodoret says,— "The great Eustathius, bishop of Antioch, who, upon the death of Philogonius, had been appointed his successor by the unanimous suffrages of the priests and of the people, and of believers, was the first to speak." Now this is doubted, for two reasons—first, because Sozomen says it was Eusebius Pamphilus; and if it had not

arose and delivered an oration in honor of the emperor, rendering thanks to God on account of him; at the conclusion of
which, he rehearsed a hymn, which he had composed to the
glory of God. When he had ceased speaking, and silence was
again restored,[1] the emperor rose and delivered himself in the
following words:

---

been Eusebius, himself, he would not have withheld the orator's name,
where he says, he, who had the first seat on the emperor's right, spoke
first; secondly, because another error is apparent in the statement of
Theodoret, namely, there was a bishop Paulinus between Philogonius
and Eustathius, the latter of whom had previously been bishop of Berea
in Syria; and he, who errs in the one part, may in the other. Gelasius
says [book II. chap. 5],— "Hosius occupied the first seat next to
Constantine" [probably on the left] "in the name of Pope Silvester."
Finally, to quote the opinion of Dr. Anthony Pagi, editor of Baronius
[edition of Lucca, 1739], in his own language, as nearly as I can
translate it,— "If there were any question as to the esteem and authority
in which any one was held, by the emperor, at this Synod, verily
Eusebius of Cæsarea, either surpassed Osius [that is, Hosius], or fully
equaled him." However, by this statement, he perhaps does not intend
to deny the former assertion of Baronius, that Hosius was presiding in
the place of the pope, Silvester. If he was sole president, it is
unaccountable that he should not have had the most honorable seat on
the right of the emperor, which certainly was not the fact. Gregory, of
Cæsarea in Cappadocia, in an oration upon the fathers of the Nicene
Synod, declares that it was neither Eusebius nor Eustathius who
delivered the first speech (this is found in the writings of Theodore, of
Mopsuestia), but Alexander of Alexandria.—*Baron, IV. 105.*

Constantine, himself, was chief President, certainly, on this great
occasion, when he occupied the golden chair. Probably on one side of
the emperor sat his Western favorite, Hosius, and on the other side his
Eastern favorite Eusebius, as the latter has several times told us. The
chair might have been partially of wood, but it was "wrought with gold."

[1]   Stanley says,— "All eyes were fixed on Constantine. He cast
round one of those bright glances of which he was master; and then,
after a momentary self-recollection, addressed them in a short speech,"
&c.   This suggestion about the "Bright glance" might be a little
improved by adding that he slightly winked one eye to Pamphilus, his
future historian. Stanley further records that the emperor spoke in Latin,
because that was the court language; but very few of the hearers could
understand him, as they were mostly Greeks.

OPENING ADDRESS OF THE EMPEROR.

"It was once my chief desire, dearest friends, to enjoy the spectacle of your united presence; and now that this desire is fulfilled, I feel myself bound to render thanks to God, the universal King, because, in addition to all His other benefits, he has granted me a blessing higher than all the rest, in permitting me to see you not only all assembled together, but all united in a common harmony of sentiment. I pray therefore that no malignant adversary may henceforth interfere to mar our happy state; I pray that, now the impious hostility of the tyrants has been forever removed by the power of God our Saviour, that spirit who delights in evil may devise no other means for exposing the divine records to blasphemous calumny; for, in my judgment, intestine strife within the Church of God is far more evil and dangerous than any kind of war or conflict; and these our differences appear to me more grievous than any outward trouble. Accordingly, when, by the will and with the cooperation of God, I had been victorious over my enemies, and thought that nothing more remained but to render thanks to Him, and sympathize in the joy of those whom he had restored to freedom through my instrumentality; as soon as I heard that intelligence which I had least expected to receive, I mean the news of your dissensions, I judged it to be of no secondary importance, but with the earnest desire that a remedy for this evil also might be found through my means, I immediately sent to require your presence. And now I rejoice in beholding your assembly; but I feel that my desires will be most completely fulfilled when I can see you all united in one judgment, and that common spirit of peace and concord prevailing amongst you all, which it becomes you, as consecrated to the service of God, to commend to others. Delay not, then, dear friends; delay not, ye ministers of God, and faithful servants of Him who is our common Lord and Saviour: begin from this moment to discard the causes of that disunion which has existed among you, and remove the perplexities of controversy by embracing the principles of peace. For by such conduct you will at the same time be acting in a manner most pleasing to the supreme God, and you will confer an exceeding favor on me, who am your fellow servant."[1]

After closing his speech and some conversational remarks, he gave strict attention to the debaters among the members of the Synod present, who spoke by turns.

"Then indeed," continues Eusebius Pamphilus, "some began to impeach their nearest associates, while others, in reply, preferred complaints against the accusers themselves.[2]

"Many topics were introduced by each party, and much controversy was excited from the very commencement, the emperor listening patiently, and, with deliberate impartiality, considering whatever was advanced. He in part supported the statements which were made on both sides, and gradually softened the asperity of those who contentiously opposed each other, conciliating each by his mildness and affability. Addressing them in the Greek language, with which he was, by no means, unacquainted, in a manner at once interesting and persuasive, he wrought conviction on the minds of some, and prevailed on others by entreaty. Those who spoke well, he applauded, and incited all to unanimity; until, at length, he brought about a similarity of judgment of all, and conformity of opinion on all the controverted points; so that there was not only unity in the confession of faith, but also a general agreement as to the time for the celebration of the salutary feast of Easter. Moreover the doctrines, which had thus the common consent, were confirmed by the signature of each individual."

----

[1]   "The emperor thus spoke in Latin," says Sozomen, "and a bystander supplied the interpretation—for the emperor was almost ignorant of the Greek."   However, Socrates declares "he was well acquainted with Greek."   See the similar statement of Eusebius. But he spoke in Latin, it being, perhaps, most familiar to him. This speech is copied from Eusebius' Life of Constantine.

[2]   Theodoret says,— "This recriminating was stopped by the emperor, who, seeing it assuming a violent character, after listening a while, interposed, and fixed another day for the discussion of their differences of this nature."   See the manner in which the emperor settled these personal quarrels at the great feast, to which he invited all the bishops of the Council, during the Vicennalia, in chap. XIV.

CHAPTER IX.

THE FINAL DELIBERATION AND DECISIONS OF THE COUNCIL UPON THE IMPORTANT QUESTIONS OF DOCTRINE. —CONSTANTINE PARTICIPATES IN THE DEBATES.—THE ARIAN CREED REJECTED.—THE HOMOOUSIAN ESTABLISHED FOREVER. —LETTERS OF THE COUNCIL AND CONSTANTINE, DESCRIBING THE UNANIMOUS DECISIONS RESPECTING THE "CONSUBSTANTIAL" CREED. —ARIUS ANATHEMATIZED AND HIS THALIA CONDEMNED; ALSO THE ARIANS BANISHED, AND THEIR WORDS PROSCRIBED BY THE EMPEROR.

Theodoret says, that the great Eustathius, in his panegyric upon the emperor, commended the diligent attention he had manifested in the regulation of ecclesiastical affairs. At the close of this speech, the excellent emperor exhorted them to unanimity and concord; he recalled to their remembrance the cruelty of the late tyrants, and reminded them of the honorable peace which God had at this period and by his means, accorded them. And he remarked, how very grievous it was, that, at the very time when their enemies were destroyed, and when no one dared to molest them, that they should fall upon one another, and afford matter for diversion and ridicule to their adversaries, while they were debating about holy things, which ought to be determined by the written word, indited by the Holy Spirit, which they possessed. "For the gospel," continued he, " the apostolical writings and the ancient prophecies clearly teach us what we are to believe concerning the Divine nature. Let then, all contentious disputation be set aside; and let us seek, in the divinely inspired word, the solution of all doubtful topics."

These and similar exhortations he, like an affectionate son, addressed to the bishops as to fathers desiring their accordance in the apostolical doctrines. Most of those present were won over by his arguments, established concord among themselves, and embraced sound doctrine. There were, however, a few, of whom mention has been already made, who sided with Arius; and amongst them were Menophantus, bishop of Ephesus; Patrophilus, bishop of Scythopolis; Theognis, bishop of Nice; and Narcissus, bishop of Neronpolis, which is a town of the second Cilicia, and is now called Irenopolis; also Theonas, bishop of Marmarica, and Secundus, bishop of Ptolemais in Egypt. They drew up a declaration of their creed, and presented it to the Council. Instead of being recognized, it was torn to pieces, and was declared to be spurious and false. So great was the uproar raised against them, and so many were the reproaches cast on them for having betrayed religion, that they all, with the exception of Secundus and Theonas, stood up and excommunicated Arius.[1] This impious man, having thus been expelled from

---

[1]   In the discussions of the Creed, there were curious scenes, according to some writers. One reports that St. Nicholas, the red-faced bishop of Myra, whom we sometimes call "Santa Claus," got so enraged at Arius, that he slapped him on the jaw. And when a song was repeated out of *Thalia*, the bishops kept their eyes fast shut and stopped their ears. When the Arian Creed, signed by 18 bishops was produced, the other 100 bishops tore it in pieces and ejected Arius from the Council. He disappeared before the close of the Council. His book, Thalia, was burnt on the spot, and so many copies were soon destroyed, that it became a very rare work. The whole Christian world has altered the Nicene Creed, in some respects, in order to make it conform to common sense, as Stanley thinks.

The statement of Athanasius is, that "Arius was anathematized, and his Thalia condemned." He was then banished into Illyricum, by the emperor, who sent edicts to all parts of his empire denouncing him and his doctrines, and even threatening those who should dare to speak well of the exiled bishops, or to adopt their sentiment. The concealment of any of his writings was made a capital crime, as Constantine's epistles will unmistakably prove.

But, in respect to the excommunication of Arius, Theodoret differs form other authorities, who are supported by many corroborating circumstances. In the words of another historian, "Although the two personal friend of Arius,—Eusebius of Nicomedia and Theognis of Nice,—subscribed the creed, which they did alone for the sake of peace, as they declared, still they refused to subscribe, with the rest, the condemnatory clauses against the Arian doctrines, because they could not believe, they said, from his written and oral teachings, that he had taught the doctrines he was accused of having inculcated."

At the time, this was overlooked in them. But subsequently they were banished, as well as Arius, to whom they had proved faithful as far as they dared. They seem, like Eusebius of Cæsarea and others, to have adopted the Nicene Creed in a sense to suit their peculiar views. This was their plea in subsequent disputes upon the subject. But their opponents charged them with duplicity and deception in the course they pursued. Even the Arian Philostorgius confesses [book I chap. 9], that all the bishops consented to the exposition of faith made at Nicæa, with the exception of Secundus and Theon. But the rest of the Arian bishops, with Eusebius of Nicomedia, whom he calls "the Great," Theognis and Tharis [Maris?] embraced the sentence of the Council with a fraudulent and treacherous purpose; for, under the term *homoousios* [of one substance with], they secretly introduced that of *homoiousios* [of like substance with]. But, Philostorgius adds, that Secundus charged Eusebius of Nicomedia with subscribing the creed to escape being sent into banishment, and predicted that, within a year, he would be banished too; which prediction proved true; for Eusebius was sent into exile in three months after the Council had adjourned, upon returning to his original Arianism.

As for Arius himself, the emperor soon recalled him from his exile in Illyricum, a country between the Adriatic and Pannonia, which is now called Dalmatia and Albania. The singular change in the emperor's disposition, and his leniency toward Arius, seem to have been effected by the influence of his sister Constantia, who was inclined to Arian principles. She was the widow of Licinius, but yet a favorite sister to Constantine; and, being removed, by death, soon after the Council of Nice, she is said to have left a strong impression on the emperor's mind, in favor of Arius, and against his banishment. Moreover, she left a friend in the imperial household, who, being a presbyter of Arian proclivities, exerted all his influence to effect the restoration of Arius, which was accomplished. The emperor's letter to Arius, was dated the 25th of November, and began as follows:— "It was intimated to your reverence, sometime since, that you might come to my court, in order to your being admitted to the enjoyment of our presence." And the letter ends thus: "May God protect you, beloved."

Arius and Euzoius came, and presented to the emperor their declaration of faith. It was as follows:— "We believe in one God, the Father Almighty, and in the Lord Jesus Christ his Son, who was made of Him before all ages; God the Word, by whom all things were made, which are in the heavens and upon the earth; who descended, became incarnate, suffered, rose again, ascended into the heavens, and will again come to judge the living and the dead. We believe, also, in the Holy Spirit, in the resurrection of the flesh, in the life of the coming age, in the kingdom of the heavens, and in one Catholic Church of God extending over the whole earth."

"This confession of faith was," says Dr. Neander, "without doubt, similar to the former one of Arius," yet it was satisfactory to the emperor, and he granted him a full pardon at once. However, the Orthodox could not be induced to receive Arius again into their favor.

the church, a confession of faith, which is received to this day, was drawn up by unanimous consent; and, as soon as it was signed, the Council was dissolved. The bishops above mentioned, however, did not consent to it in sincerity, but only in appearance. . . . . . Eustathius, of Antioch, afterwards wrote against them, and confuted their blasphemies.

The remarks of Socrates on this head are, that "some of the bishops scoffed at the word *Homoonsios* (consubstantial), and would not subscribe to the condemnation of Arius. Upon which the Synod anathematized Arius and all who adhered to his opinions, at the same time prohibiting him from entering into Alexandria.[1] By an edict of the emperor, also, Arius, himself, was sent into exile, together with Eusebius [of Nicomedia] and Theognis;[2] but the two latter, a short time after their banishment,

---

Athanasius refused to admit him to communion at Alexandria, in spite of the commands of Constantine himself.

Arius regarded the Holy Spirit as being the first created nature, produced by the Son of God, He placed the same distance betwixt the Son and the Holy Spirit, which he had supposed between the Father and the Son.—*See Athan. Orat.* I. c. *Arian.* * G.

[1]   That is from entering the city in an official capacity. The *Homoousian* dogma was firmly established, in spite of all Arian influence, and Gibbon declares that "the consubstantiality of the Father and the Son was established by the Council of Nice, and has been unanimously received as a fundamental article of the Christian faith, by the consent of the Greek, the Latin, the Oriental, and the Protestant churches."—*See Decline and Fall,* II. 21.

[2]   Philostorgius says, in his history, that the emperor punished them because, while they subscribed to the Homoöusian faith, they entertained sentiments at variance with it; and that he recalled Secundus and his associates from banishment, and sent letters in every direction exploding the term *Homoousios,* and confirming the doctrine of a diversity of substance.   This is doubtless exaggeration.   However, Athanasius asserts, that Constantine opposed the *Homoousian*; although, at the Nicene Synod, he favored it, as Eusebius positively declares.

Eusebius, of Nicomedia, Maris and Theognis were banished, by an imperial decree, a short time after the Council, for some overt acts displaying Arian sentiments.   But, according to Philostorgius, they were recalled, after a period of three years, by command of the emperor; and they immediately put forth a form of faith, and sent it in every direction,

tendered a written declaration of their change of sentiment, and concurrence in the faith of the substantiality of the Son with the Father. The Synod, also, with one accord, wrote an epistle to the Church of the Alexandrians, and to the believers in Egypt, Libya, and Pentapolis."

In this letter are the following sentences: "It was unanimously decided by the bishops, assembled at Nice, that this impious opinion of Arius should be anathematized, with all the blasphemous expressions he has uttered, in affirming, that *the Son of God sprang from nothing, and that there was a time when he was not; saying, moreover, that the Son of God was possessed of free-will, so as to be capable either of vice or virtue; and calling him a creature and a work.* All these sentiments the holy Synod has anathematized. So contagious has his pestilential error proved, as to involve, in the same perdition, Theonas, bishop of Marmarica, and Secundus of Ptolemais; for they have suffered the same condemnation as himself."[1]

"It should be here observed," says Socrates, "that Arius had written a treatise on his own opinion, which he entitled 'Thalia;'[2]

---

in order to counteract the Nicene Creed. Their written retraction, as quoted by Socrates, contains these words:— "If ye should now think fit to restore us to your presence, ye will have us on all points conformable, and acquiescent in your decrees. For, since it has seemed good to your piety to deal tenderly with, and recall, even him who was primarily accused; it would be absurd for us to be silent, and thus submit to presumptive evidence against ourselves, when the one, who was arraigned, has been permitted to clear himself from the charges brought against him."

[1]   See the same letter as quoted by Theodoret, who renders it somewhat differently from Socrates, though not very essentially so.

[2]   This work was written by Arius subsequently to his excommunication by the Alexandrian Synod of A.D. 321, according to some authorities. Philostorgius says, he wrote also a collection of songs for sailors, millers, and pilgrims,—an old expedient for spreading religious opinions among the common people, as Neander observes. Milman, in Gibbon's Rome, notes the fact thus: "Arius appears to have been the first, who availed himself of this means of impressing his doctrines on the popular ear, beguiling the ignorant, as Philostorgius terms it, by the sweetness of his music, into the impiety of his doctrines."

According to Sozomen, "Arian singers used to parade the streets of Constantinople by night, till Chrysostom arrayed against them a band of Orthodox choristers."—*See B.*, VIIII. *chap.* 8.

St. Ambrose composed hymns in Latin to the glory to the Trinity, for the people to sing in churches, A.D. 374.—*See Bingham's Antiquities of the Christian Church.*

An old rhetorican at Rome, named Fabius Marius Victorinus, composed hymns to advance the Orthodox Trinitarian cause. The following lines are the beginning of one of old Victorinus' hymns, as I find them printed in *Patrologiæ,* VIII. 1159:

HYMNUS PRIMUS

Adesto, lumen verum, pater omnipotens, Deus.
Adesto, lumen luminis, mysterium et virtus Dei.
Adesto, sancte spiritus, patris, et filii copula.
Tu cum quiescis pater es, cum procedia, filius.
In unum qui cuncta nectis, tu es spiritus sanctus,
Unum primum, unum a se ortum, unum ante unum Deus.

Translation:

HYMN FIRST.

Be present, true light, father almighty, God.
Be present, light of light, wonder and excellence of God.
Be present, holy spirit, bond of father and son,
You, when you rest, are the father, when you go forth, the son.
You, who are joined the whole in one, are the holy spirit,
The primal one, one from himself arisen, the one prior to one, God.

This Victorinus, according to St. Jerome, was the "vice-consul of the African nation," and taught rhetoric, principally at Rome under Constantine. In his extreme old age, he received the faith of Christ, which was not long prior to A.D. 362. He wrote books against the doctrines of the Manichæans, and commentaries of the apostolical Scriptures. He held a controversy with the Arian, Candidus, on the divine generation of the Word; and his four books against the Arians, besides several epistles to Candidus, are preserved in Patrologiæ, vol. VIII., together with the opposing arguments of Candidus. The following is the beginning of the latter's book on the divine generation, addressed to "Marius Victorinus, the rhetorican":—

but the character of the book was loose and dissolute, its style and metres not being very unlike the songs of Sotadés, the obscene Maronite.[1] This production the Synod condemned at the same time.

"All generation, O my dear old Victorinus, is a change of some kind. But, as to divinity, God is evidently wholly immutable. However, God, as he is the first cause of all things, so he is the father in respect to all things. If, therefore, God is unchangeable and immutable, inasmuch as he is unchangeable and immutable, he is neither begotten nor made. So, therefore, it stands thus: God is unbegotten. For, indeed, generation is such in consequence of conversion and mutation. But no substance, nor ingredients of substance, nor existence, nor qualities of existence, nor existing things, nor attributes of existing things, nor power, could there have been prior to God. For what is superior to God? Whether a power or existence or substance or *on*?"

The reply of Victorinus, addressed to Candidus, the Arian, begins thus:— "Is it your great intelligence, O noble Candidus, which has so fascinated me? To say of God, that man is above him, would be audacious. But as, indeed, the *nous ethikos* (moral sense) was put into our soul, and the breath of life was sent, from above, unto the forms of intelligence inscribed from eternity upon our souls the elevation of our souls may re-mould the ineffable things even into investigable mysteries of God's volitions and operations. For he is willing to be seen, yea, even now, in respect to what kind of situation his person is in, which, of itself, is difficult to be comprehended; but, declare,— is it impossible?"

[1] Maronite, that is a follower of John Maro, the monk.—*See Decline and Fall, chap.* 47, § 3.

"It was undoubtedly the same Sotadés, to whom Martial refers, in the following epigram upon a certain class of pretenders to the classical rank.—*See Martial's Epigrams, book* II.

"As I ne'er boast the back-turned verse
Nor bawdy Sotadés rehearse,
Whom Greekish echo nowhere quotes
In all her loose, pedantic notes;
Nor have, from Attis, art so fine,
To frame the Choliambic line,
Thanks to the Galliambon sweet
For classic rank and measure meet,
Though, claiming not a perfect style,
I'm not a bard so very vile."

"The emperor also wrote to the Church of the Alexandrians: 'The splendor of truth has dissipated, at the command of God, those dissensions, schisms, tumults, and, so to speak, deadly poisons of discord. I assembled, at the city of Nice, most of the bishops; with whom I, myself, also, who am but one of you, and who rejoice exceedingly in being your fellow-servant, undertook the investigation of the truth. Accordingly all points which seemed, in consequence of ambiguity, to furnish any pretext for dissension, have been discussed and accurately examined. Let us, therefore, embrace that doctrine which the Almighty has presented to us.'

"Constantine wrote another letter, addressed to the bishops and the people, in which he says: 'If any treatise composed by Arius should be discovered, let it be consigned to the flames, in order that not only his depraved doctrine may be suppressed, but, also, that no memorial of him may be, by any means, left. This, therefore, I decree, that, if any one shall be detected in concealing a book compiled by Arius, and shall not instantly bring it forward and burn it, the penalty for this offence shall be death. May God preserve you."

"The bishops, who were convened at the Council of Nice," continues Socrates, "after settling the Arian question, drew up and enrolled certain other ecclesiastical regulations, which they are accustomed to term canons,[1] and then departed to their respective cities."

An abstract of these canons will be given in a subsequent chapter.

This is my rendering from the Latin of Baronius. Sotadés was an Egyptian poet, who composed verses, which, when read backwards, had an obscene meaning. Athanasius seems to have been the first that called Arius a "Sotadeän writer,—probably because there was a double meaning to some of his hymns, the second signification being more strongly Arian than the first appearance.

[1] See Hammond's Canons of the Church, p. 15, Oxford edition, 1843, and Beveridge's Pandecta Canonum, tom. I, 58; also Thomas Attig's Historia Concilii Niceni, published at Leipsie, in 1712, etc.

CHAPTER X.

THE PASTORAL LETTER OF EUSEBIUS PAMPHILUS,[1] OF CÆSAREA. CONCERNING THE SAME THINGS, WITH OTHER CIRCUMSTANCES.

"It is likely that you have learnt, from other sources, what was decided respecting the faith of the church at the general Council of Nice; for the fame of great transactions generally precedes the accurate detail of them. But, lest rumors not strictly founded in truth should have reached you, I think it necessary to send to you, first, the formulary of faith originally proposed by *us*; and, secondly, the additions appended to it by the bishops when setting it forth. The following is *our* formulary, which was read in the presence of our most pious emperor, and which was fully approved by all: [2]

" 'The faith which we hold is that which we have received from the bishops who were before us,[3] and in the rudiments of

---

[1] This letter I copy from Theodoret, who says, in introducing it: "The following letter was written by Eusebius, bishop of Cæsarea, to some of the Arians, who had accused him, it seems, of treachery. They had previously honored him, because he had adopted their sentiments." But the fact is, he sent this letter to his own diocesans, as several contemporary writers tell us.—*See the statement of Athanasius.*

[2] In the copy of this letter given by Socrates, the words here used are, it "seemed to meet with universal approbation."

[3] Origen says, in reference to those who declare Christ to be God, "Aiming to honor Christ, they teach what is untrue of him." He denies the doctrine of the Patripassians, who believed that the Logos (the Word) is the Eternal Father. He taught that the Son is, in God, what reason is in man, and that the Holy Spirit is nothing else but the divine energy or power of acting and working. In describing the nature of Christ, Origen and other early fathers quoted the prophets to prove what the connection was between the Father, Son, and Holy Ghost. They assumed that Jesus was the Christ, the Messiah predicted, and wherever a passage of Scripture, or any old sacred book, seemed to refer to him, they felt sure it was good, sound evidence, fit to found their dogmas upon. Origen uses highly poetical language in describing Christ, such as he found in some of the prophets.—*See Principiis, chap. 2.* He taught

which we were instructed when we were baptized. It is that which we learnt from the Holy Scriptures, and which, when among the presbytery as well as when we were placed in the episcopal office, we have believed, and have taught; and which we now believe, for we still uphold our own faith. It is as follows:

" 'I believe in one God, the Father Almighty, the Maker of all things, whether visible or invisible; and in one Lord Jesus Christ, the Word of God, God of God, Light of Light, Life of Life, the only begotten Son, the First-born of all creatures, begotten of the Father before all ages; by whom all things were made; who, for our salvation, took upon him our nature, and dwelt with men. He suffered and rose again the third day, and ascended to the Father; and he will come again in glory to judge the living and the dead. We also believe in one Holy Ghost. We believe in the existence of each person; we believe that the Father is in truth the Father; that the Son is in truth the Son; that the Holy Ghost is in truth the Holy Ghost; for our Lord, when sending out his disciples to preach the gospel, said, 'Go forth and teach all nations, baptizing them in the name of the Father, and of the Son, and of the Holy Ghost. We positively affirm that we hold this faith, that we have always held it, and that we shall adhere to it even unto death, condemning all ungodly heresy. We testify, as before God the Almighty and our Lord Jesus Christ, that we have believed in these truths from the heart and from the soul, ever since we have been capable of reflection; and

---

that prayers should be addressed only to the Father, *chap.* 6, * 3. He said the love and wisdom of God in Christ was what made them one, *chap.* 6, § 4. Justin Martyr taught that the Logos emanated from God, being his self-manifestation, as a personality derived from God's essence, and ever intimately united with Him by this community of essence. Some of the learned bishops had probably deduced their theories from these great sources.

Constantine believed that the generation of the Son was not material, but intellectual. Being the Word, that is, the wisdom, of God, he did not diminish the substance of the Father by his descent, anymore than a word from our lips diminishes our wisdom.—*See his "Oration to the Saints."* chap 3.

we have the means of showing, and, indeed, of convincing you, that we have always. during all periods, believed and preached them.'

"When this formulary was set forth by us, no one found occasion to gainsay[1] it; but our beloved emperor was the first to testify that is was most orthodox, and that he coincided in opinion with it; and he exhorted the others to sign it, and to receive all the doctrine it contained, with the single addition of the word consubstantial. He said that this term 'consubstantial' implied no bodily affection, for that the Son did not derive of his existence from the Father either by means of division or abscission. 'An immaterial, intellectual, and incorporeal nature,' said he, 'cannot be subjected to bodily operations. These things must be understood as bearing a divine and mysterious signification.' Thus reasoned our wisest and most religious emperor. The omission of the word *consubstantial* was adopted as the pretext for composing the following formulary:

THE ARTICLE OF FAITH MAINTAINED BY THE COUNCIL.[2]

"We believe in one God, the Father Almighty, the Maker of all things, visible and invisible. And in one Lord Jesus Christ, the Son of God, the only begotten of the Father; he is begotten, that is to say, he is of the substance of God, God of God, Light of Light, very God of very God, begotten and not made, being

---

[1] In Socrates, the words of this letter are, "When these articles of faith were proposed, they were received without opposition; nay, our most pious emperor himself was the first to admit that they were perfectly orthodox, and that he precisely concurred in the sentiments contained in them; exhorting all present to give them their assent, and subscribe to these very articles. It was suggested, however, that the word homoöusios (consubstantial) should be introduced, an expression which the emperor himself explained. . . . And the bishops, on account of the word *Homoosius*, drew up the formula of faith which was finally adopted.

[2] Dean Stanley says, "The Creed of the Council of Nice is the only one accepted throughout the Universal Church, and this Council alone, of all ever held, still retains a hold on the mass of Christendom."

of one substance with[1] the Father; by whom all things, both in heaven and on earth, were made. Who for us men, and for our salvation, came down from heaven, and took our nature, and became man; he suffered, and rose again the third day; he ascended into heaven, and will come to judge the living and the dead. And we believe in the Holy Ghost. The holy catholic and apostolical church condemns all those who say that there was a period in which the Son of God did not exist; that before he was begotten, he had no existence; that he was called out of nothing into being; that he is of a different nature and of a different substance from the Father; and that he is susceptible of variation or of change."[2]

"When they had set forth this formulary, we did not fail to revert to that passage in which they assert that the Son is of the substance of the Father, and of one substance with the Father. Questions and arguments thence arose. By investigating the meaning of the term, they were led to confess that the word *consubstantial* signifies that the Son is of the Father, but not as being part of the Father's nature. We deemed it right to receive this opinion; for that is sound doctrine which teaches that the

---

[1] Of one substance with, or "consubstantial." The Greek word used here was *homoousios*. Philostorgius, the Arian, says (book I chap. 7), that before the Synod was held at Nice, Alexander, Bishop of Alexandria, came to Nicomedia [where the emperor resided], and after a convention with Hosius, of Cordova, and the other bishops who were with him, prevailed upon the Synod to declare the Son "consubstantial with" the Father, and to expel Arius from the communion of the church. Dr. Neander remarks, that perhaps there may be some truth in this; but he declares further, that Athanasius was probably the soul of the *Homoousian* party. Gibbon calls Hosius, or "Osius," as he writes it, the father of the Nicene Creed. It is certain that Hosius was in great favor with the emperor, whom Eusebius represents as introducing, or first advocating, the HOMOÖUSIAN, a word already familiar to the Platonists, according to Gibbon. But Athanasius denies that Constantine favored the Homoöusian.

[2] There are many copies of this Nicene Creed extant among the writings of the early fathers, but they are nearly all of precisely the same purport as this.

There are two prominent points in this creed: first, Christ's real divinity and equality with the Father; secondly, his personal distinction from the Father.

Son is of the Father, but not part of his substance. From the love of peace, and from the fear of deviating from the principles of truth, we accept this exposition without rejecting the term in question. For the same reason we admit the expression, *begotten, but not made;* for they say that the word *made* is applied to all things which were created by the Son, and which cannot be placed in comparison with him —none of the creatures that he has made being like him. He is by nature superior to all created objects, for he was begotten of the Father, as the Holy Scriptures teach, by a mode of generation which is incomprehensible and inexplicable to all created beings. The mode in which the Son is said to be of the substance of the Father, was declared to bear no relation to the body, nor to the laws of mortal life. It was also shown that it does not either imply division of substance, nor abscission, nor any change or diminution in the power of the Father.

"The nature of the unbegotten Father, is not susceptible of these operations. It was concluded that the expression *of the substance of the Father*, implies only that the Son of God does not resemble, in any one respect, the creatures which he has made; but that to the Father, who begat him, he is in all points perfectly similar; for he is of the nature and of the substance of none save of the Father. This interpretation having been given of the doctrine, it appeared right to us to receive it, especially as some of the ancient and most celebrated bishops and writers have used the term consubstantial when reasoning on the Divinity of the Father and of the Son.

"These are the circumstances which I had to communicate respecting the formulary of the faith. To it we all agreed, not thoughtlessly, but after mature reflection; and after having subjected it to thorough examination, in the presence of our most beloved emperor, we all, for the above reasons, acquiesced in it. We also willingly submitted to the anathema appended by them to their formulary of faith, because it prohibits the use of words which are not scriptural,—for almost all the disorders and troubles of the church have risen from the introduction of such words. As no one part of the inspired writing contains the assertion that the Son was called out of nothing into being, or that there was a period in which he had no existence, nor, indeed, any of the other phrases of similar import which have been introduced, it does not appear reasonable to assert or to teach such things. In this opinion, therefore, we judged it right to agree; and, indeed, we had never, at any former period, been accustomed to use such words.[1] . . . . . .

"And here our most beloved emperor began to reason concerning the Son's divine origin, and his existence before all ages. 'He was power in the Father, even before he was begotten,—the Father having always been the Father, just as the Son has always been a King and Saviour; he has always possessed all power, and has likewise always remained in the same state.'

"We thought it requisite, beloved brethren, to transmit you an account of these circumstances, in order to show you what examination and investigation we bestowed on all the questions which we had to decide; and also to prove how firmly, even to the last hour, we persevered in refusing our assent to certain sentences, which when merely committed to writing, offended us. But yet we subsequently, and without contention, received these very doctrines, because, after thorough investigation of their signification, they no longer appeared objectionable to us, but seemed conformable to the faith held by us and confessed in our formulary."

---

[1] The statement that follows next is omitted by me, because its authenticity is very doubtful, it being omitted by Socrates and Epiphanius. The purport of it is, that, during the debate in the Council of Alexandria, A.D. 321, at which Arius was first anathematized, Alexander seemed to incline first to one party and then to the other; but finally declared himself in favor of the "consubstantial" and "co-eternal" dogma.

CHAPTER XI.

ACCOUNTS FROM EUSTATHIUS CONCERNING THE SAME THINGS; ALSO FROM ATHANASIUS, OF ALEXANDRIA, AS QUOTED IN THEODORET'S HISTORY OF THE CHURCH.

Eustathius,[1] bishop of Antioch, the Great, says; "When the bishops, assembled at Nice, began to inquire into the nature of the faith, the formulary of Eusebius was brought forward, which contained undisguised evidence of his blasphemy. The reading of it occasioned great grief to the audience, on account of the depravity of the doctrines; and the writer was covered with shame. After the guilt of the partisans of Eusebius had been clearly proved, and the impious writing torn up in sight of all,[2] some amongst them, under the pretence of preserving peace, imposed silence on those who usually manifested superior powers of eloquence.

---

[1] Eustathius was a native of Side in Pamphylia. Being bishop of Berea (now Aleppo) in Syria, he was promoted, by the Nicene Council, to the patriarchate of Antioch. He was banished, A.D. 330, on account of his opposition to Arianism, into Thrace, where he died about A.D. 360. He was highly esteemed by the Orthodox, and took a leading part in the Council of Nice—delivering either the first, or one of the first, addresses in praise of the emperor before this great Synod. He wrote eight books against the Arians, some of which still exist, and may be seen in *Fabricii Biblioth. Græca, vol.* VIII

[2] See the pastoral letter of Eusebius, of Cæsarea, *ante.* His account of the reception of *his* proposed formulary is contrary to this statement of his warm opponent, Eustathius. The account of Eusebius is evidently most worthy of credit, from corroborating circumstances, and as appears by the statements of Athanasius. It was the tendency of the Eastern church, whose bishops were there in great numbers, to favor the Eusebian theory, both then and subsequently. But there is some reason to doubt which Eusebius is referred to here by Eustathius. It is possible he refers to the bishop of Nicomedia; for the latter, according to Ambrose (book III chap. 7, De Fide), had endeavored to defend the Arian conception of the Son of God.—*See the letter of Arius to Eusebius of Nicomedia.*

"The Arians, fearing lest they should be ejected from the church[1] by so numerous a Council of bishops, proceeded at once to condemn the doctrines objected to, and unanimously signed the confession of faith. They contrived, however, to retain their principal dignities,[2] although they ought rather to have experienced humiliation. Sometimes secretly, and sometimes openly, they continued to vindicate the condemned doctrines, and brought forth various arguments in proof of them. Wholly bent upon establishing these false opinions, they shrank from the scrutiny of learned men, and, indeed, of all who are capable of investigation; and they manifested great animosity against professors of religion. But we do not believe that these atheists can overcome God."

Thus far I quote from the great Eustathius.

Athanasius,[3] who was equally zealous in the cause of religion, and who was the successor in the ministry of the cele-

---

[1] "Ostracized" is the literal meaning of this phrase.

[2] Their bishoprice.

[3] Alexander, bishop of Alexandria, dying on the sixth day of February, A.D. 326, only a few months after the Council of Nice, was succeeded by Athanasius, the Great.

This last named intrepid supporter of the Nicene Creed was born at Alexandria, A.D. 296 and died the second day of May A.D. 373. He ever took the lead in the Arian controversy, sometimes triumphing, and at others suffering from the accusations of his opponents. At the Council of Tyre, A.D. 325, he answered to the charges of murder, unchastity, necromancy, encouraging sedition, oppressive exactions of money, and misuse of church property. His works are chiefly controversial. In those directed against Arius and Arianism, I find, some quotations from the book called "Thalia," which the Nicene Council condemned, as Athanasius and Socrates report. That work was probably written after A.D. 321, the date of the Synod of Alexandria, which first excommunicated Arius for heresy.

SENTENCES FROM THALIA

Thalia means "The Banquet." Only fragments of this work are extant, and they are in the works of Athanasius. Thalia was partly in prose and partly in verse.

Athanasius quotes passages, as follows: "God has not always been Father; later he became so. The Son is not from eternity; He came from nothing. When God wished to create us, He first created a being

brated Alexander, communicated the following intelligence in the letter addressed to the Africans:—

"The bishops,[1] being convened to the Council were desirous of refuting the impious assertions of the Arians, that the Son

---

which He called the Logos, Sophia, and Son, who should create us as an instrument.

"There are two Sophias: one is God (*i.e.*, endiathetos), by which even the Son was made. It is only by sharing the nature of this inner Sophia of God that the Son was also called Wisdom. So, also, besides the Son, there is another Logos—he who is God; as the Son participates in this Logos, He also is by grace called Logos and Son."

"The Logos does not perfectly know the Father. He cannot entirely understand his own nature. The substance of the Father, the Son, and the Holy Ghost are entirely different, the one from the other.

"These three persons are, in their essence, thoroughly and infinitely dissimilar.

"God is ineffable, and nothing (therefore not even the Son) is equal to or like Him, or of the same glory.

"This eternal God made the Son before all creatures, and adopted Him for His Son. The Son has nothing in his own nature skin to God, and is not like to Him in essence."—*Clark's Hefele.*

SENTENCES FROM ATHANASIUS.

Athanasius, in different parts of his works, above mentioned, expresses the following ideas, which will show how he was accustomed to argue certain points of doctrine, et. Speaking of Arius, he says,— "He vomits forth the poison of impiety." "The Nicene fathers, hearing his impiety, closed their ears." "He trusts in the violence and the menaces of Eusebius." "He puts forth the Thalia in imitation of the filthy Sotadés." "He draws up a rescript of faith for Constantine, in which he conceals the venom of heresy, by usurping the naked words of Scripture." "He dies by a sudden, miraculous death, on the Sabbath day," and "His death is an argument against the Arian heresy." "Arius, the Sotadeän." "Arius, the Atheist." "Arius is like the serpent that deceived Eve." "The devil is the father of the Arian heresy." "The Thalia is of an effeminate style, being written in imitation of Sotades, an Egyptian poet." "Thalia is accustomed to be sung among tipplers."—*See the complete extant works of St. Athanasius, Archbishop of Alexandria, edited by J. P. Migne, from which I translate.*

[1] Eusebius, it will be noticed, gives great prominence to the influence of the emperor in this discussion, representing everything as proceeding from him, while Athanasius does not even mention it. Each

was created out of nothing; that he is a creature and created being; that there was a period in which he did not exist; and that he is mutable by nature.

"They all agreed in propounding the following declarations, which are in accordance with the Holy Scriptures; namely, that the Son is by nature the only begotten Son of God, the Word, the Power, and the Wisdom of the Father; that he is, as John said 'very God,' and, as Paul has written, 'the brightness of the glory, and the express image of the person of the Father.' (Heb. i. 3.)

"The followers of Eusebius, who were led by evil doctrines, then assembled for deliberation, and came to the following conclusions: We are also of God. 'There is but one God of whom are all things.' (1 Cor. vi. 8.) 'Old things are passed away; behold all things are become new, and all things are of God.' (2 Cor. v. 17, 18.) They also dwelt particularly upon the following doctrine, contained in the Book of the Pastor: 'Believe above all that there is one God, who created and restored all things, calling them from nothing into being.'

"But the bishops saw through their evil design and impious artifice, and gave a clearer elucidation of these words, by explaining them as referring to God, and wrote that the Son of God is of the substance of God; so that while the creatures, which do not in any way derive their existence of, or from, themselves, are said to be of God, the Son alone is said to be of the substance of the Father; this being peculiar to the only begotten Son—the true Word of the Father. This is the reason why the bishops were led to write, that he is of the substance of the Father.

"The Arians, who seemed few in number, were again interrogated as to whether they would admit the following points of doctrine: 'That the Son is not a creature, but the Power, and the Wisdom, and likewise the Image, of the Father; that he is eternal—in no respects differing from the Father, and that he is very God.' It was remarked, that the Eusebians signified to each

---

probably felt at liberty to recount those things most agreeable to his party interests; or else, to suppress what seemed to him unimportant.

other by signs, that these declarations were equally applicable to us; for it is said that we are the image and the glory of God. This is said of us because we are living beings. There are (to pursue their train of argument) many power; for it is written, 'All the powers of God went out of the land of Egypt.' (Exod. xii. 41.) The canker-worm and the locust are said to be great powers. (Joel ii. 25.) And elsewhere it is written, 'The God of powers is with us; the God of Jacob is our helper.' For we are not merely children of God, but the Son also calls us brethren. Their saying that Christ is God in truth, gives us no uneasiness; for he was true, and he is true.

"The Arians made false deductions; but the bishops, having detected their deceitfulness in this matter, collected from Scripture those passages which say of Christ that 'He is the glory, the fountain, the stream, and the figure, of the substance,' and they quoted the following words; 'In thy light we shall see light;' and likewise, 'I and the Father are one.' They then clearly and briefly confessed that the Father and the Son are of the same substance; for this, indeed, is the signification of the passages which have been mentioned. The complaint of the Arians, that these precise words are not to be found in the Scripture, is a vain argument; and it may besides be objected to them, that their impious assertions are not taken from Scripture; for it is not written that the Son was created, and that there was a period in which he did not exist. And also, that they themselves complain of having been condemned for using expressions, which, though certainly not scriptural, are yet, they say, consonant with religion. They drew words from the dunghill, and published them upon earth.

"The bishops, on the contrary, did not invent any expressions themselves; but, having received the testimony of the fathers, they wrote accordingly. Indeed, formerly, as far back as about one hundred and thirty years, the bishops of the great city of Rome, and of our city,[1] disproved the assertion, that the Son is a creature, and that he is not of the substance of the Father. Eusebius, bishop of Cæsarea, is acquainted with these facts. He,

---

[1] Dionysius, the bishop of Rome, and Alexander, of Byzantium.

at one time, favored the Arian heresy; but he afterwards signed the confession of faith of the Council of Nice. He wrote a letter to inform his diocesans,[1] that the word 'consubstantial' is found in certain ancient documents, and is used, by illustrious bishops and learned writers, as a term for expressing the Divinity of the Father and of the Son.

"Some of the bishops, who had carefully concealed their obnoxious opinions, consented to coincide with the Council when they perceived that it was very strong in point of numbers.[2] Theonas and Secundus, not choosing to dissimulate in the same way, were excommunicated, by one consent, as those who esteemed the Arian blasphemy above evangelical doctrines. The bishops then returned to the Council, and drew up twenty laws to regulate the discipline of the church."

---

[1]   See this epistle in the narrative from Socrates. It is commonly called the "Pastoral Letter of Eusebius Pamphilus," being addressed to those whose pastor he was; i.e. the Cæsareans.

[2]   At first, seventeen bishops, who probably belonged to the strictly Arian party, declined to go with the majority; among them, Eusebius of Cæsarea, who, on the first day after they were presented, absolutely refused his assent to them, according to the account Athanasius. It should be understood, as Rufinus says (I. 5), that all who refused their assent, were threatened with the loss of their places, and condemnation as refractory subjects. Besides, as Eusebius declares in his pastoral letter, Constantine explained the *Homoousian*, himself, and his interpretation of it was not against the theory of the subordination of Christ to the Father. Afterwards, the emperor, when he found the term generally interpreted differently, displayed his dislike of it. But what Constantine most desired, was conformity and union among the churches, that would add strength to his empire. Eusebius and the Arian bishops accepted the *Homoousian* ("of the same substance") as a designation of the likeness in respect to essence; that is, that Christ is like God in respect to essence, though subordinate to Him.— *Neander Ch. Hist.* II 377.

CHAPTER XII.

DISCIPLINARY LAWS DISCUSSED. —THE CELIBACY OF THE CLERGY
PROPOSED. —THIS QUESTION SETTLED IN FAVOR OF HONORABLE
MARRIAGE. —CERTAIN CANONS DECREED AND ESTABLISHED.

Sozomen says: "With the view of reforming the life and
conduct of those, who were admitted into the churches, the
Synod enacted several laws which were called canons. Some
thought that a law ought to be passed, enacting, that bishops and
presbyters, deacons and sub-deacons, should not cohabit with
the wife espoused before they had entered the priesthood. But
Paphnutius, the confessor [that is, one who had confessed, even
under torture, that he was a believer in the Christian faith,] stood
up and testified against this proposition. He said, that marriage
was honorable and chaste, and advised the Synod not to frame a
law which would be difficult to observe, and which might serve
as an occasion of incontinence to them and their wives; and he
reminded them, that, according to the ancient tradition of the
church, those, who were unmarried when they entered the
communion of sacred orders, were required to remain so, but,
that those who were married, were not to put away their wives.
Such was the advice of Paphnutius, although he was, himself,
unmarried; and, in accordance with it, the Synod refrained from
enacting the proposed law, but left the matter to the decision of
individual judgment."

THE MELETIANS DEGRADED, ETC.

It was decreed, that Meletius[1] might remain in his own city,
Lycus, but not hold any power, either for laying on of hands, or

---

[1]   Concerning Meletius and his schism we have the following
accounts:
      He was ordained a bishop, and dwelt in the city of Lycus, called
also Lycopolis, in the Thebaid (now included in Egypt). In rank, he

stood next to the bishop of Alexandria, and was in high repute until a little while before A.D. 306, when he began to disseminate the doctrine that all, who had violated, in any way, their fidelity to the Christian faith under persecutions,—that is, who had denied the faith to escape punishment,—ought to be excluded from the fellowship of the Church until the perfect restoration of peace (this being a time of persecution), and then, upon sincere contrition, to be shown by proper penances, they might first obtain forgiveness from the Church. But Peter maintained that it was not advisable to wait for the end of the persecution, and that the repentant should at once be admitted to suitable penances, and so be restored.

Now it appears, from the account of Socrates, who certainly was no apologist of Meletius, that Peter, bishop of Alexandria, had once taken refuge in flight from his persecutors, although he subsequently suffered martyrdom, under Diocletian, A.D. 311, being suddenly seized and beheaded, according to Eusebius, "as if by the order of Maximin."

Whether the flight of Peter gave rise to the Meletian schism does not appear, although Socrates says that, during Peter's absence after his flight, Meletius usurped the right of ordaining in his diocese.

But, on the other hand, Peter, upon his return, tried Meletius on many charges, one of which was, that, during the persecution, he had *denied* the faith and sacrificed, that is, to the gods, for which conduct, "the most holy Peter," says Theodoret, "deposed him and convicted him of impiety." "But," says Socrates (book I chap. 6), "he pretended, that, as an innocent man, he had been unjustly dealt with, loading Peter with calumnious reproaches." Theodoret adds, moreover, that he excited troubles and commotions in Thebes and in the countries around Egypt, and sought the chief power in Alexandria. However, it is generally admitted by friends and foes both, that there were many persons among the Meletians eminent for the piety of their lives.

At the request of Alexander, of Alexandria, just before the assembling of the Council of Nice, he (Meletius) prepared a breviary containing a list of his adherents among the clergy, &c.; mentioning, by name, twenty-eight bishops, four presbyters, and five deacons, some of them noted men, and Harpocration, Theodore, Theon of Nelups, etc.— *See Baronius*, IV. 129, *with Pagi's notes.*

It was the custom, when any episcopal seat became vacant, for the bishops of the province, in the presence of the people, to elect and ordain a successor. But Meletius was accustomed to ordain bishops, presbyters, and deacons of his own authority.— *See Epiphanius, de Hæres*, 68.

Epiphanius, whose book is here referred to, was a Christian writer, born about 320, at Besanduce, a village of Palestine. He spent his

to bestow any ecclesiastical office upon any one, or to go into any other country, nor to stand in a favorable light in his own city; that he might retain only the dignity and name of the office; but, otherwise, that those who had been appointed by him presbyters, as he pretended, after being confirmed by a more solemn ordination, might be admitted into the communion of the Church on this condition: "to be sure," such were the words of the Synod, "they may hold the rank of the ecclesiastical dignity and ministry, but yet, they are to be inferior, in all respects, to all the presbyters in every province, and, to those clergymen who, turning back again, shall have been ordained by that most honorable man, our colleague, Alexander."[1]

THE BOOK OF JUDITH APPROBATED, AS SACRED.

"The great Council computed the Book of Judith," says St. Jerome, "among the number of the sacred Scriptures, as we glean from history." This book was placed by the Hebrews among the *Hagiographa*; that is, those Scriptures which belonged neither to the penteteuch nor the prophetical books.[2]

---

youth among the monks of Egypt, but returned and founded a monastery near his native village, and presided over it. About 367 he was elected bishop of Salamis, afterwards called Constantia, in Cyprus. He was a bitter opposer of Origen's sentiments. He died in 403. His principal work is his account of the different heresies, before and after, the coming of our Saviour.

Athanasius was a bitter foe to the Meletians, probably because they espoused the Arian cause. All that the Council of Nice punished Meletius for, was because he created separate churches, and ordained bishops and clergymen over them not under the See of Alexandria, and not holding communion with the Catholics.

[1]   See the synodical epistle sent to the Church of Alexandria. Theodoret says this letter was sent from the Council to the Alexandrian Church; but he does not state how it was despatched thither, or at what precise day, during the synodical deliberations, it was written. The object of it was, he says, to inform that church, what had been decreed respecting the Meletian innovations.

[2]   There is a false tradition handed down to us, that this great first Council of the Christian bishops decreed what books of the Bible should be held canonical. Other councils passed such decrees.

THE CREED OR FORMULARY[1] OF FAITH ESTABLISHED

BOOKS OF THE BIBLE

The first Synod at which the books of the Bible were made the subject of a special ordinance was that of Laodicea, but the precise date of this Synod, as well as the integrity of the canon in question, has been warmly debated. — *See Wescott on the New Test. Canon.*

This Synod of Laodicea in Phrygia, held about 363, enacted sixty Canons, which are still extant in their original Greek. — *See Beveridge's Pandecta Canonum.*

The 60th Canon is as follows:

These are all the books of the Old Testament, which may be read aloud: Genesis, Exodus, Leviticus, Numbers, Deuteronomy, Joshua, Judges, Ruth, Esther, First and Second Books of Kings, Third and Fourth Books of Kings, First and Second Books of Chronicles, First and Second Books of Ezra, the Book of the one hundred and fifty Psalms, the Proverbs of Solomon, Ecclesiastes, the Song of Songs, Job, the twelve Prophets, Isaiah, Jeremiah and Baruch, the Lamentations and Letters, Ezekiel and Daniel.

The books of the New Testament are these: Four Gospels according to Matthew, Mark, Luke and John; the Acts of the Apostles; the Seven Catholic Epistles, namely, one of James, two of Peter, three of John, one of Jude; the fourteen Epistles of Paul, one to the Romans, two to the Corinthians, one to the Galatians, one to the Ephesians, one to the Philippians, one to the Colossians, two to Thessalonians, one to the Hebrews, two to Timothy, one to Titus, and one to Philemon

SYNOD AT HIPPO
A Full Council of All Africa

This place, in Africa, was called Hippo Regius. Aurelius, Archbishop of Carthage since 391, presided.

St. Augustine was then a priest at Hippo, and delivered his discourse, "Of the faith and the Symbol," which is preserved in his writings.

[1]This is usually called the "Symbol," or the "Confession of Faith." It is stated in Baronius, that Hosius drew up and exhibited this symbol, which was approved by the suffrages of the Nicene Synod.— *See his Eccl. Annals, vol.* IV

The date of the Nicene formulary, inscribed on the document, was the nineteenth day of June, A.D. 325.

They enacted forty-one Canons. The thirty-sixth was as follows:

Besides the Canonical Scriptures, nothing shall be read in the Church under the title of "divine writings." The Canonical books are: Genesis, Exodus, Leviticus, Numbers, Deuteronomy, Joshua, Judges, Ruth, the four Books of Kings, the two Books of Chronicles, Job, the Psalms of David, the five books of Solomon, the Prophets, Isaiah, Jeremiah, Daniel, Ezekiel, Tobias, Judith, Esther, two Books of Esdras, two of Maccabees.

The Books of the New Testament are: The Four Gospels, the Acts of the Apostles, thirteen Epistles of Paul, one Epistle of Paul to the Hebrews, two Epistles of Peter, three of John, one of James one of Jude, and the Revelation of John.

Concerning the confirmation of this Canon, the Church on the other side of the sea shall be consulted.

The acts of martyrs shall also be read on their anniversaries.

The reports of discussions at this Synod were all lost, only abridgments of their acts being now extant.

There was a work translated into Latin about the year A.D. 500, by Dionysius the Less, of Rome, which was called "The Apostolical Canons," an old Greek collection of uncertain date and authorship, but supposed to have been used early in the fourth century. It contained eighty-four Canons. (*Bev. Pandecta Canonum.*) The style of the work is that of the third century. The origin of most of these Canons is unknown. However, they were derived partly from the Synods of the Church. The eighty-fourth Canon says that the books which were held venerable and sacred by all our clergy and laity, are as follows:

Of the Old Testament: The five books of Moses, Joshua, Judges, Ruth, four Books of Kings, two of Chronicles, Esdras, Esther, Judith, three of Maccabees, Job, one hundred and forty Psalms, three books of Solomon, Proverbs, Ecclesiastes, the Song of Songs, sixteen Prophets, the Wisdom of Sirach.

Of the New Testament: The Four Evangelists, Paul's fourteen Epistles, two of Peter, three of John, one of James, one of Jude, two of Clement, the Constitutions of the Churches and the Acts of the Apostles.—*Hefele.*

Dr. Von Drey, author of a learned work upon these Canons, thinks this eighty-fourth the least ancient of any of them. Some writers call this the eighty-fifth instead of eighty-fourth Canon.

Mosheim says (*Eccl. Hist., book* I *chap.* 2, *sec.* 19), "The Apostolic Canons are eighty-five ecclesiastical laws, and exhibit the principles of

We believe in one god, the Father Almighty, the Maker of all
things visible and invisible; and in one Lord Jesus Christ, the

---

discipline received in the Greek and Oriental Churches, in the second
and third centuries.

"The eight Books of Apostolic Constitutions are the work of some
austere and melancholy author, who designed to reform the worship and
discipline of the Church, which he thought were fallen from their
original purity and sanctity, and who ventured to prefix the names of the
apostles to his precepts and regulations, in order to give them currency."

The book of the Shepherd of Hermas, was so called, because an *angel*
in the form and habit of a shepherd, is the leading character in the
drama.   The author is unknown.   "If he was indeed sane," says
Mosheim, "he deemed it proper to forge dialogues held with God and
angels, in order to insinuate what he regarded as salutary truths more
effectually into the minds of his readers.   But his celestial spirits talk
more insipidly than our scavengers and porters."

Clement, who became Bishop of Rome A.D. 101, used the following
books of the New Testament: 1 Corinthians, Ephesians, 1 Timothy (?)
Titus (?), Hebrews and James.

Ignatius (107) used: 1 Corinthians, Ephesians, Philippians (?), 1
Thessalonians (?) and Philemon (?).

Polycarp (160) used Romans, 1 Corinthians, 2 Corinthians, Galatians,
Ephesians, Philippians, 1 Thessalonians (?), 1 Timothy, 2 Timothy, 1
Peter, 1 John.

Barnabas (60) used Matthew, 1 Timothy (?), 2 Timothy (?).

Origen (215), according to Wescott, above quoted, used Matthew,
Mark, Luke, John.   He adopted most of the books of our present Canon.
But he denied that Paul wrote Hebrews, although the thoughts of that
epistle were perhaps Paul's and written by some one who had been
intimate with Paul, either Clement, Bishop of Rome, or Luke, the
author of Acts.   He also considered some other books true and inspired,
of which were the Epistle of Barnabas; the Doctrine of Peter; the Book
of Enoch, and the Pastor of Hermas.

Athanasius rejected the book of Esther.

The Council of Carthage, A.D. 397, adopted the same rule as that of
Hippo; however, ranking Hebrews among Paul's fourteen Epistles.   Pope
Innocent I., a few years later, confirmed this catalogue of sacred books
by a decree, which finally decided the Canon of the Latin Church.

But the Synod of Aix, A.D. 789, would exclude the Apocalypse.
Martin Luther excluded Hebrews, James, Jude, and the Apocalypse.
The Council of Trent merely confirmed the Canon of Hippo.— *New Am.
Cyclopedia.*

Son of God, the only begotten of the Father. He is begotten, that is to say, he is of the substance of God, God of God, Light of Light, very God of very God, begotten and not made, being of one with[1] the Father; by whom all things, both in heaven and on earth, were made. Who, for us men, and for our salvation, came down from heaven, and took our nature, and became man. He suffered, and rose again the third day. He ascended into heaven, and will come to judge the living and the dead. And we believe in the Holy Ghost.[2]

HYMN TO GOD DECREED.

A certain hymn to the glory of God was decreed and established by the Nicene Synod, which, as Sozomen seems to think, the Arians took the liberty to alter and corrupt. He says, "The Catholics had been accustomed, according to ancient tradition and common usage, to sing, 'Gloria Patri et Filio, et Spiritui Sancto,' whereas the Arians, in baptizing, used the form following: 'Gloria Patri per Filium in Spiritu Sancto.' "

CELEBRATION OF THE PASCHAL FESTIVAL: THAT IS THE PASSOVER,[3] COMMONLY CALLED EASTER.

The Council assigned the first Sunday after the fourteenth moon following the vernal equinox for the celebration of the Passover in all the Christian countries everywhere, —this day having been proposed by Alexander, the bishop of Alexandria in Egypt, which nation was considered "the most skillful as to the course of the stars."[4]

---

[1] The word used here was *homoousios* which, in Latin, is *consubstantialis*, and, in English, *consubstantial with.*

[2] See the pastoral letter of Eusebius of Cæsarea.

[3] The day in remembrance of Christ's dying and expiating the sins of men, was called the Passover or Easter (Pascha) because they supposed that Christ was crucified on the same day in which the Jews kept their Passover—*Mosheim.*

[4] This time was not founded upon a true and accurate calculation. Pope Gregory XIII. reformed and corrected it, A.D. 1582. Easter is the first Sunday after the first full moon that occurs after the 21st day of March.

THE TWENTY CANONS OF THE COUNCILS OF NICE.

The principal substance and purport of these synodical decrees are here copied and translated from the various Latin authors, who have tried to collect and explain as much of them as could be found extant.

"In the first place the impiety," as the Synod termed it, "of Arius having been condemned, as well as his blasphemous sentiments,"[1] the Council proceeded to settle the Meletian question, and, then, that of the Paschal Festival, and, finally, that of the Novatian schism etc.,[2] enacting, also, twenty canons, in the following order:—

1. Forbidding the promotion in the church of self-made eunuchs:

Against Ordaining a Self-Mutilator.

The language of the Council's decree was, "If any has been deformed by physicians on account of a physical infirmity, or has been mutilated by barbarians, he may, nevertheless, remain among the clergy. But, if any, being sane, has dismembered himself, it becomes necessary, both that he should be prohibited from being established among the clergy,[3] and that no such one should be successively promoted." However, if the evidence showed clearly that the mutilation was not a self-infliction, but was done by certain others (either barbarians, or masters) daring to effect it, the decree specified, that, if they had come in most

---

[1]   See the synodical epistle to the Alexandrian Church, for the particular heresy of Arius, and in what it consisted, as the Synod conceived.

[2]   See also the letter of Constantine to those bishops who were not present, concerning the matters transacted by the Council of Nice.

[3]   Leontius, the Arian, being thus unhappily self-mutilated, was deposed from the grade of a presbyter, becoming, subsequently, conspicuous for Arian principles.

worthy persons in other respects, the rule should be to receive them into the clerical order.[1]

2. Forbidding the hasty ordination of new converts to Christianity:

Admission and Promotion of Gentiles.
"Whereas, very many, either compelled by necessity or otherwise, had acted against the welfare of the church by following the former rule, namely, that persons having only recently acceded to the church from the life of a Gentile, might, after being instructed a little while, be led to the spiritual bath, and at the same time that they were baptized, might be advanced to the episcopate or presbytery," therefore the Council declared it would be most agreeable to their wishes that this rule should be dispensed with, and not be followed in respect to any others. For they thought "there was need of time, both for one who was to be catechised, and, after baptism, as much more time, for his probation.

"For it is a wise saying of the apostle, as follows: " 'Not a novice, lest through pride he fall into condemnation, and into the snare of the devil.' If hereafter a cleric is guilty of a grave offense, proved by two or three witnesses, he must resign his spiritual office. Any one who acts against this ordinance, and ventures to be disobedient to this great Synod is in danger of being expelled from the clergy."

3. Forbidding the clergy to keep female friends in their houses.

Against the Admission of Women as Sorores.
"The Council decreed that it should not be permitted to a bishop, or to a presbyter, or to a deacon to have the legal privilege of introducing to his house, or receiving a woman intro-

---

[1] See Matt. xix. 12. Many, in those early times, and among them even the great Origen, construing this passage literally, emasculated themselves in order to avoid temptation.

duced by others, unless she were his mother or sister, or aunt, or, at least, such as had escaped suspicion."

In the first ages of the Church, some Christians, clergymen and laymen, contracted a sort of spiritual marriage with unmarried ladies, so that they lived together; and there was a friendly connection between them for their mutual religious advancement. They were known by the name of *subintroducta*, or the Greek *suneisaktoi*, and sisters. That which began in the spirit, however, in many cases, ended in the flesh. —*Hefele.*

4. That ordinations shall be performed by, at least, three bishops:

Ordination of Bishops.

All the bishops in a province shall unite to constitute and ordain a bishop. But if this is inconvenient, through great necessity or the length of the journey, three, at least, shall be present to ordain a candidate, and then it shall be necessary, that those absent shall consent thereto by letter. The conformation of these proceedings belongs to the metropolitan bishop.

5. That an excommunication of either a clergyman or a layman, by the sentence of a single bishop, shall be valid everywhere, till it shall be decided by a provincial council, which shall be held twice a year, the first before Lent, and the second in the autumn.

6. Gives superiority to the bishop of Alexandria over the bishops and churches of Egypt, Libya, and Pentapolis, also, to the patriarchs of Rome and Antioch, precedence, and, to metropolitans, a veto power over all elections to the episcopal office within their provinces:

Concerning the Primacy of certain Churches.

"Whereas, the Roman Church has always held the first rank, but likewise Egypt holds the same, therefore the bishop of Alexandria may have power over all the Egyptian provinces; since this is the rule in respect to the Roman church. For the same reason, he, who has been established among the Antiochian churches, and, moreover, in the other provinces, the churches of the larger cities may hold the primacy. But, throughout all, let it be understood, that if any one has been ordained before it was agreeable to the metropolitan bishops, he ought not to be a bishop (because the holy Synod has ordained this to be so). Assuredly, it will be seen, if reasonably weighed by the common understanding, that, according to the ecclesiastical rule, two or three bishops, obstinately opposing, may be counteracted, and overruled in the regular mode. Let that judgment prevail, which shall have been esteemed right by the majority."

7. Gives to the bishop of Ælia the rank of a metropolitan.

Primacy of the Ælian Church.

Since an ancient custom has obtained and a venerable tradition, that deference should be paid to the bishop of Ælia[1](that is, Jerusalem), therefore let him retain this, his special honor, but, also, to the metropolitan, may be preserved the dignity which belongs to him.[2]

8. Permits Novatian bishops and clergymen to be restored on certain conditions:

Novations permitted to return to the Catholic Church.

Concerning the Novatian schismatics, [3] the Council decreed, that, if any of them had been willing to come over to the

---

[1]   Jerusalem having been destroyed by Titus, a colony was subsequently established on its ruins by Adrian, and named "Ælia." It was under the jurisdiction of Cæsarea, the metropolis of Palestine.

[2]   The Roman prelate probably exercised, through his legates, Vito and Vincentius, and, also, his particular friend, Hosius, great influence in the Council of Nice. In a letter from the Synod, dated 8 Kalen. Novem., it is stated that Pope Silvester's advice, and his position respecting the Trinity, were fully concurred in by the Synod, and all his views adopted.

[3]   This canon I find in Baronius, tom. iv., anno 325, cap. 142.

Catholic Church, they might be re-ordained, and so remain among the clergy. "But, before all this, they shall make a confession (which ought to be set forth in writing), that they ought to commune with, both those who have entered upon a second marriage, and those, who, in time of persecution, have lapsed from the faith, to whom yet, although fallen, there is a time fixed, and a season appointed, for repentance; that, in all things, they may observe the decrees of the Catholic Church. And wherever any one of them may be found, whether in village or

---

The Novatian party had their name from Novatus, who is styled by the Roman Catholics, the first anti-pope, and is called by the Latin writers "Novatian." Philostorgius says he was a native of Phrygia. He was of heathen parentage, and was educated a philosopher of the sect of Stoics. He was chosen bishop of Rome, by some bishops upon the death of Fabianus. But Cornelius was chosen at the same time by a larger number of bishops, and hence there was a division in the church. His adversaries called his followers, sometimes "Cathari," that is, Puritans, by way of derision. These Novatians obliged such as came over to them from the other party of Christians, to submit to a re-baptism. In Phrygia, they condemned second marriages; at Constantinople, they had no certain rule as to this; while in the West, they received bigamists to communion without scruple.

Sozomen says, "It is related that the emperor, under the impulse of an ardent desire to see harmony re-established among Christians, summoned Acesius, bishop of the Novatians, to the Council, placed before him the exposition of the faith and of the feast [Passover], which had received the signature of the bishops, and asked whether he could agree thereto. Acesius answered, that their exposition involved no new doctrine, and that he accorded in opinion with the Synod, and that he had, from the beginning, held these sentiments with respect both to the faith and the feast. 'Why, then,' asked the emperor, 'do you keep aloof from communion with others, if you are of one mind with them?' He replied, that the dissension first broke out under Decius, between Novatus and Cornelius, and that he considered such persons unworthy of communion, who, after baptism, had fallen into those sins, which the Scriptures declare to be unto death; for, that the remission of those sins, he thought, depended on the will of God, and not on the priests. The emperor replied by saying, 'O Acesius, take a ladder, and ascend alone to heaven!'"

Sozomen elsewhere remarks, that Acesius was much esteemed by the emperor on account of his virtuous life.

city, ordained by Catholics, so shall he remain among the clergy, yet every one, in his own order. But, if any of them come to a place where there is a bishop or presbyter, of the Catholic Church, it is evident that the *bishop* of the Catholic Church shall have his own proper episcopal dignity. So, likewise, the *presbyter* and *deacon* shall each have the same. But whoever may come from among them [Novatians], if a bishop, he may have the dignity of a presbyter, unless, indeed, it may please the Catholic bishop to accord to him even the honor of the episcopal name. However, if otherwise, he shall provide for him the place of a country bishop (chorepiscopou) or of a priest, that he may, by all means, appear to be in the number of the clergy, and that there may not be two bishops in one city.

9 and 10. That presbyters, who had lapsed, or committed crimes before their ordinations, such as would disqualify them for the sacred office, should be deprived of their offices, as soon as discovered.[1]

11. Required those, who had lapsed during the late persecutions under Licinius, first, to do pennance at the threshold of the church three years; secondly, in the porch among the catechumens, seven years; and, thirdly, to be allowed to witness, but not join in, the celebration of the eucharist, for two years more.

12. That the greater apostates shall also spend ten years in the second penance, but this to be at the discretion of the bishops. "Those, who, being called by grace, have been zealous, and have laid aside their belts, used in the armies of Licinius, but afterwards put them on again, and even given money to be admitted again into his service, shall remain three years among the *hearers*, and ten among the lower rank. But in case of these

---

[1]   In the ninth canon, I find these words: "Si quis ergo fuerit fornicationis damnatus, sive antequam consecraretur, sive postea, deponitur."— *Bev. Pand. Canonum, tom:* I

According to St. Ambrose, the Council of Nice decreed, that no one whatever ought to be clergyman, who had boldly contracted a second marriage.

penitents, their intentions and the nature of their penitence must be judged. The real penitents, who show it by tears and fear and good works, after finishing their penance among the hearers, may, perhaps, take part among those that pray; and the bishop may show them even greater lenity."

13. That a dying penitent may receive the sacrament:

Communion at the Point of Death.
"Concerning those who die, the ancient and ecclesiastical law shall now be observed, that, if any one is about to expire, he may not be deprived of the viaticum of the Lord. But if, in despair of life, having received the communion, and partaken of the offering, he be again numbered with the living, let him be placed with those who participate in prayer only. By all means, however, let the bishops impart the offerings to every one, on examination, who desires, at the point of death, to partake of the eucharist."

14. Lapsed catechumens are to spend three years in the first stage of penance, *i.e.*, as hearers. After that they can then join in prayer with the other catechumens.

15. That bishops, presbyters, and deacons shall remain in their own several churches, and not go to others.

16. That presbyters and deacons, forsaking their own churches and going to others, must be sent back; and a bishop shall not ordain those under another bishop without the latter's consent.

17. All clergymen, who loan money, or goods, on interest, to be deposed, and their names struck off the list.

18. Deacons shall not present the bread and wine to the presbyters, or partake thereof themselves, or sit among the presbyters:

Deacons not to Deliver the Eucharist to Presbyters.
"It having come to the knowledge of the great and holy Council, that, in certain places and cities, the eucharist is administered, by deacons, to presbyters, and neither law nor custom permitting that those, who have no authority to offer the body of Christ, should deliver it to those who have; and it being also understood, that some deacons receive the eucharist before even the bishops, let, therefore, all these irregularities be removed, and let the deacons remain within their own limits, knowing that they are ministers of the bishops, and inferior to the presbyters. Let them receive the eucharist in their proper place, after the presbyters, whether it be administered by a bishop or presbyter. Nor is it permitted to deacons to sit among the presbyters, as that is against the rule and order. If any one will not obey, even after these regulations, let him desist from his ministry."[1]

19. The followers of Paul, of Samosata,[2] on returning to the church, to be re-baptized, and re-ordained if they are to become clergymen.

20. Kneeling at prayers on the Lord's Day, and from Easter to Pentecost, disapproved.[3] "On the Lord's Day, and on the days of Pentecost, all shall offer their prayers to God standing."

---

[1] Deacons had the administration of the offerings, and of all the temporal concerns of the churches. They were employed to carry the bread and wine, says Justin Martyr, to such communicants as were absent. The poor received alms from their hands, and the clergy their stipends and remuneration.

[2]Paul, of Samosata, was a bishop of Antioch in Syria, A.D. 269, who taught the heresy, that there is but one God, called in the Scriptures, the Father; and, that Christ was only a mere man, endowed with the Divine *Word* or *Wisdom.* This Paul held his church at Antioch under Zenobia, Queen of Palmyra, until she was conquered by Aurelian.

[3] Murdock's notes to Mosheim's Institutes, vol. I Many other canons have been attributed to the Council of Nice by certain writers, but their genuineness is not admitted by Protestants.

"Constantine the Great solemnly confirmed the Nicene Creed, immediately after it had been drawn up by the Council, and he threatened all such as would not subscribe to it with exile. At the conclusion of the Synod he raised all the decrees of the assembly to the

CHAPTER XIII.

THE LETTER DESPATCHED FROM THE COUNCIL OF NICE TO THE CHURCH
OF ALEXANDRIA —STATEMENT OF WHAT HAD BEEN DECREED
AGAINST THE INNOVATIONS OF MELETIUS, AS WELL AS THE COUNCIL'S
OPINION OF ARIUS AND HIS PARTICULAR HERESIES.

THE SYNODICAL EPISTLE.

"To the Church of Alexandria, which, by the grace of God,
is great and holy, and to the beloved brethren in Egypt, Libya,
and Pentapolis, the bishops who have been convened to the great
and holy Council of Nice, send greeting in the Lord.

"The great and holy Council of Nice having been convened
by the grace of God, and by the appointment of the most religious emperor, Constantine, who summoned us from different
provinces and cities, we judge it requisite to inform you by letter
what we have debated and examined, decreed and established.

"In the first place, the impious perverseness of Arius, was
investigated before our most religious emperor, Constantine.[1]

---

[1]   This is unmerited adulation.   Constantine, although he exhibited
much zeal for all the concerns of the Church, had never, as yet, received
baptism, and continued to remain without the pale of the community of
believers, being only a catechumen.

Neander says, "It is most probable that, carrying his heathen
superstition into Christianity, he looked upon baptism as a sort of rite for
the magical removal of sin, and so delayed it, in the confidence that,
although he had not lived an exemplary life, he might yet, in the end, be
enabled to enter into bliss, purified from all his sins."   Even Eusebius of
Cæsarea, his contemporary historian and panegyrist, says he suffered
persons to abuse his confidence with indescribable hypocrasy."

The heathen writers of his time say. that, having inquired of a Platonic
philosopher what he could do to atone for his crimes, it was replied to him,
that there was no lustration for such atrocious conduct.   However, when he
had become very sick and near to death, A.D. 337, he was baptized by
Eusebius, bishop of Nicomedia, who had influenced him to favor the Arians
in his last years, and to banish many Orthodox bishops.

In the Encyclopedia Americana, Gibbon is said to have best described
the character, influence, and policy of Constantine, of all who have
attempted it.   According to this historian he was brave, a favorite of his

His impiety was unanimously condemned, as well as the blasphemous sentiments which he had propounded for the purpose of dishonoring the Son of God, alleging that he was created; that before he was made he existed not; that there was a period in which he had no existence; and that he can, according to his own free-will, be capable either of virtue or of vice. The holy Council condemned all these assertions, and impatiently refused to listen to such impious and foolish opinions, and such blasphemous expressions.

"The final decision concerning him you already know, or will soon hear; but we will not mention it now, lest we should appear to trample on a man who has already received the recompense due to his sins. Theonas, bishop of Marmarica, and Secundus, bishop of Ptolemais, have, however, been led astray by his impiety, and have received the same sentence. But, after we had, by the grace of God, been delivered from these false and blasphemous opinions, and from those persons who dared to raise discord and division among a once peaceable people, there yet remained the temerity of Meletius, and of those ordained by him.

"We shall now inform you, beloved brethren, of the decrees of the Council on this subject. It was decided by the holy Council, that Meletius should be treated with clemency, though, strictly speaking, he was not worthy of the least concession. He was permitted to remain in his own city,[1] but was divested of all

---

he was baptized by Eusebius, bishop of Nicomedia, who had influenced him to favor the Arians in his last years, and to banish many Orthodox bishops.

In the Encyclopedia Americana, Gibbon is said to have best described the character, influence, and policy of Constantine, of all who have attempted it. According to this historian he was brave, a favorite of his people, and a terror to his foes; fond of the sciences, as well as of arms, and gave them both his protection. But his zeal for Christianity was excited not less by the knowledge, that the religion, which was embraced by a majority of the Roman empire, must prevail, and the strength of the government must be increased by protecting it, than by a wish to apply its consoling powers to the relief of a heavy conscience.— *See decline and Fall of the Roman Empire, vol.II., chap. 20.*

[1] Lycopolis, but Sozomen calls it "Lycus". It is now called "Sioot," and is the principal town of Upper Egypt.

power, whether of nominating or of ordination, neither was he to exercise those functions in any province or city; he only retained the mere title and the honor of the episcopal office. Those who had received ordination at his hands, were to submit to more holy re-ordination; they were to be admitted to communion, and were to receive the honor of the ministry; but, in every diocese and church, they were to be accounted inferior to those who were ordained before them by Alexander, our much honored fellow-minister. It was decreed that they should not elect or nominate, or, indeed, do anything without the consent of the bishops of the Catholic and Apostolical Church, who are under Alexander. But those who, by the grace of God, and in answer to prayer, have been preserved from schism, and have continued blameless in the Catholic and Apostolical Church, are to have the power of electing, and of nominating, those who are worthy of the clerical office, and are permitted to do everything that accords with law and the authority of the Church.

"If it should happen, that any of those now holding an office in the church should die, then let those recently admitted be advanced to the honors of the deceased, provided only that they appear worthy, and that the people choose them, and that the election be confirmed and ratified by the Catholic bishop of Alexandria. This same privilege has been conceded to all the others. With respect to Meletius, however, an exception has been made, both on account of his former insubordination, and the rashness and impetuosity of his disposition; for, if the least authority were accorded to him, he might abuse it by again exciting confusion.

"These are the things which relate to Egypt, and to the holy Church of Alexandria. If any other resolutions were carried, you will hear of them from Alexander, our most honored fellow-minister and brother, who will give you still more accurate information, because he, himself, directed, as well as participated in, everything that took place.

"We must also apprise you, that, according to your prayers, we were all of one mind respecting the most holy paschal feast, so that our brethren of the East, who did not previously celebrate the festival as the Romans, and as you, and, indeed, as all have done from the beginning, will henceforth celebrate it with you.

"Rejoice, then, in the success of our undertakings, and in the general peace and concord, and in the extirpation of every schism; and receive, with the greatest honor and the most fervent love, Alexander, our fellow-minister and your bishop, who imparted joy to us by his presence, and who, at a very advanced period of life, has undergone so much fatigue for the purpose of restoring peace among you. Pray for us all, that what we have equitably decreed, may remain steadfast, through our Lord Jesus Christ, being done, as we trust, according to the good-will of God and the Father in the Holy Ghost, to whom be glory forever and ever. Amen."

EPISTLE OF THE EMPEROR TO THOSE BISHOPS WHO WERE NOT PRESENT.[1]

"Constantine Augustus to the churches.

"Viewing the common prosperity enjoyed at this moment as the result of the great power of divine grace, I am desirous that the blessed members of the Catholic Church should be preserved in one faith, in sincere love, and in one form of religion, towards Almighty God.

"But, because no firmer or more effective measure could be adopted to secure this end, than that of submitting each holy mode of worship to the examination of all, or most of all, the bishops, I convened as many of them as possible, and took my seat among them as one of yourselves; for I will not deny that truth which is the source of the greatest joy to me, namely, that I am your fellow-servant. Every doubtful point obtained a careful investigation, until doctrines pleasing to God and conductive to unity were fully established, so that no room remained for division or controversy concerning the faith.

The commemoration of the paschal feast[2] [Easter] being then debated, it was unanimously decided that it should every-

---

[1] From Theodoret, Bohn's new edition.
[2] There were great disputes in the early church about the proper time for celebrating the paschal solemnity (Easter), some local churches observing it on a fixed day each year, and others, with the Jews, on the fourteenth day of the new moon. A decree was issued by Pope Pius, about A.D. 147, commanding all Christians throughout the world to observe the paschal festival on a Sunday. But the bishop of

where be celebrated on the same day. It was, in the first place, declared improper to follow the custom of the Jews in the celebration of this holy festival. Let us, then, have nothing in common with the Jews, who are our adversaries. Another way has been pointed out by our Saviour. . . . . Therefore this irregularity must be corrected, in order that we may no more have anything in common with the parricides and the murderers of our Lord.

Receive, then, willingly, the one regulation unanimously adopted in the city of Rome, throughout Italy, in all Africa, in Egypt, Spain, Gaul, Britain, Libya, Greece, in the diocese of Asia and of Pontus, and in Cilicia.[1]

Smyrna came to Rome and alleged that the opposite custom of the Asiatic churches had come down to them by tradition from St. John, and the rest of the apostles. The matter was finally settled by the Nicene Council against the practice of the Eastern Church.

[1] See the canon regulating the time for celebrating Easter.

CHAPTER XIV.

THE EMPEROR'S KINDNESS TO THE BISHOPS AT THE VICENNALIA.
—HIS ENTERTAINMENT OF THEM.— HE KISSES THEIR WOUNDS.
—HIS MUNIFICENCE. — HE SETTLES THEIR PERSONAL DIFFICULTIES IN A
PECULIAR WAY. — HIS ADMONITIONS TO THEM.
—CONCLUSION. —EPILOGUE.

Those who attended the Council were three hundred and
eighteen in number; and, to these, the emperor manifested great
kindness, addressing them with much gentleness, and present-
ing them with gifts. He ordered numerous seats to be prepared
for the accommodation of all during the repast to which he invited them. Those, who were the most worthy, he received at
his own his table, and provided other seats for the rest.
Observing that some among them had had the right eye torn out,
and learning that this suffering had been undergone for the sake
of religion, he placed his lips upon the wounds, believing, that
blessing would thence result. After the conclusion of the feast,
he again presented other gifts to them. He then wrote to the governors of the provinces [or other officers],directing, that money
should be given in every city to orphans and widows, and to
those who were consecrated to the divine service; and he fixed
the amount of their annual allowance more according to the impulse of his own generosity, than to the exigencies of their
condition. . . .

Some quarrelsome individuals wrote accusations against
certain bishops, and presented the catalogue of crime to the emperor. This occurring before the restoration of concord, he received the lists, formed them into a packet to which he affixed
his seal, and put them aside. After a reconciliation had been effected, he brought out these writings and burnt them in their
presence, at the same time declaring, upon oath, that he had not
even read them. He said that the crimes of priests ought not to
be made known to the multitude, lest they should become an occasion of offence or of sin. He also said, that if he had detected a

bishop in the very act of committing adultery, he would have thrown his imperial robe over the unlawful deed, lest any should witness the scene, and be thereby injured.[1]

THE VICENNALIA.—CONSTANTINE INVITES THE BISHOPS TO GREAT FEAST. —HE ADMONISHES THEM TO BE UNANIMOUS AND DILIGENT.—PRESENTS GIFTS TO THEM, AND BIDS THEM ALL FAREWELL.

"At the very time that these decrees were passed by the Council," says Sozomen, "the twentieth anniversary of the reign of Constantine was celebrated; for it was a Roman custom to have a feast on each *tenth* year of every reign.[2]

"The emperor, therefore, invited the bishops to the festival [to which they all came[3]], and he presented suitable gifts to them; and when they were prepared to return home, he called them all together, and exhorted them to be of one mind, and at peace among themselves, so that no dissensions might henceforth creep in among them. After many other similar exhorta-

---

[1] Theodoret's Ecclesiastical History.

[2] Pamphilus says: "When the emperor held the banquet with the bishops, among whom he had established peace, he presented it, through them, as it were, an offering worthy of God. No one of the bishops was excluded from the imperial table. The proceedings on this occasion were sublime beyond description. The soldiers of the emperor's body-guard were drawn up before the door of the palace with their bare swords. The men of God (the bishops) passed along undaunted between their files into the interior of the palace. Some sat at the same table with the emperor himself; the others at side tables. One might easily imagine that one beheld the type of Christ's kingdom."—*Life of Constantine, book* III *chap.* 15.

At the festival, Eusebius Pamphilus, himself pronounced an oration and panagyric upon the emperor, in his most florid style.

It was, doubtless, now about the twenty-fifth day of July, because that is known to have been the anniversary day of Constantine's accession to the imperial throne. It could not have been earlier, but might have been a little later, as the emperor might possibly have delayed the vicennalia through deference to the bishops of the great Council.

[3] This remark I quote from Eusebius' Life of Constantine, book III. chap. 15.

tions, he concluded by commanding them to be diligent in prayer for himself, his children, and the empire, and then bade them farewell."

CONCLUSION.[1]—CONSTANTINE EXPRESSES MUCH JOY AT THE SUCCESS OF THE COUNCIL, AND ORDERS LARGE SUMS OF MONEY TO BE DISTRIBUTED.

"When matters were arranged, the emperor gave them permission to return to their own dioceses. They returned with great joy, and have ever since continued to be of one mind, being so firmly united, as to form, as it were, but one body. Constantine, rejoicing in the success of his efforts, made known these happy results, by letter, to those who were at a distance.[2] He ordered large sums of money to be liberally distributed, both among the inhabitants of the provinces and of the cities in order that the twentieth anniversary of his reign might be celebrated with public festivities."[3]

Arius, upon his excommunication at Alexandria in 321, retired to Palestine, and wrote various letters to men of distinction, in which he labored to demonstrate the truth of his doctrines, thereby drawing over immense numbers to his side, and particularly Eusebius, Bishop of Nicomedia, a man of vast influence. These bishops held a council in Bithynia, probably at Nicomedia, in which two hundred and fifty bishops are reported to have been present. All we know of their acts and decisions is, that they sent letters to all the bishops of Christendom, entreating them not to exclude the friends of Arius from their communion, and requesting them to intercede with Alexander that he would not do so.

---

[1] This additional account is from Eusebius Pamphilus.
[2] See the epistle of the emperor, pp. 111, 112.
[3] Theodoret adds, "Although the Arians impiously gainsay, and refuse to give credit to the statements of the other fathers, yet they ought to believe what has been written by this father [Eusebius], whom they have been accustomed to admire."

This first Arian Council has often been overlooked by the modern writers, or confounded with that of Antioch, A.D. 330. Sozomen mentions it, in book I. chap. 15.[1]

Arius, described by some writers as distinguished for beauty, grace, learning, and eloquence, and by others as every way ugly, though by no means ignorant and immoral, had, perhaps, imbibed his idea of the nature of Christ from Lucian, of Antioch, who suffered martyrdom in 312. After the Council of Nice, discontent with its decisions began soon to appear, and spread even back to Alexandria, in spite of Constantine's earnest efforts to check it. Alexander died, and Arius was recalled from banishment. Athanasius, now on the throne of Alexander, peremptorily refused to admit Arius as a presbyter, or allow him to enter Alexandria. For this, Athanasius was himself deposed and banished. Constantine then ordered Arius (A.D. 336) to present himself to Alexander, the Bishop of Constantinople, for recognition as a presbyter. The Orthodox prelate refused, but the emperor resolutely fixed a day when Arius *should* be recognized. Alexander prayed publicly in the church, that God would interpose in his favor. The same evening, Arius suddenly fell dead of a colic or cholera,—some say by poison, and others, that it was what Alexander prayed for.[2] But his doctrines spread more rapidly after his death than before.

The Arian contests, as was to be expected, produced several new sects. Some persons, while eager to avoid and confute the opinions of Arius, fell into opinions equally heretical. Others,

---

[1] Dr. Murdock, in Mosheim.

[2] According to Athanasius and Sozomen, Arius was passing through the city with a company of friends, and when near Constantine's forum, he stepped into a privy, such as were for public use, leaving his attendants waiting at the door. But not coming out, they looked in and found him dead, with protrusion of the bowels. It was the opinion of his friends, that he had been killed by sorcery, that is, witchcraft. We should not suspect that, but rather poison, in these days. Such murders were common. When Constantine died, his brothers and two nephews were murdered because the nephews were, by his will, made participators in the government with three sons.—*See Tillemont's Hist. Roman Empire.*

after treading in the footsteps of Arius, ventured on far beyond him, and became still greater heretics. Among these was Apollinaris, the younger, who almost set aside the human nature of Christ. He was one of the many Christian fathers, who, in that age, were very much attached to Platonism. In the same class was Marcellus, of Ancyra, who so explained the Trinity as to fall into Sabellianism. At the Nicene Council he was a prominent opponent of Arius. His pupil, Photinus, of Sirmium, taught another heresy; namely, that the Father, the Son, and the Holy Spirit are only one person, and that the Word is neither a substance nor a person.

Eusebius, of Nicomedia, the friend and protector of Arius, was maternally related to the Emperor Julian. Such was his zeal in his defense of Arius, that the Arians were often called Eusebians. Soon after the death of Arius, Alexander, of Constantinople, died, and Eusebius procured his own election to that vacant See, in defiance of the Nicene canon against translations from one See to another. He was the great leader of the Arians until his death, about 342. His history must be gathered from the writings of his religious opponents, except what is extant of Philostorgius' account of him.

Macedonius, bishop of Constantinople, a great Semi-Arian teacher, founded the sect of the Pneumatomachi, who held that the Holy Spirit is a divine energy diffused throughout the universe, and not a person distinct from the Father and the Son. This doctrine Macedonius taught during his exile, after his deposition from office by the Council of Constantinople, A.D. 360.

The three principal classes of Arians at this time were the old genuine Arians, the Semi-Arians, and the Eunomians.

Athanasius, after many trials, flights, restorations, controversies, with both the Arians and Meletians combined; and after triumphs, and persecutions, finally was firmly established upon his high throne, as shepherd and guardian of the universal church; but soon died, at Alexandria, exchanging his earthly mitre, 2 May, 373, for a crown of glory, in the seventy-eighth year of his age, having held the episcopacy forty-six years, of which twenty had been passed in exile.

Athanasius, of Anazarbus, the Arian bishop, who was present at the Nicene Council, had, in 331, the notorious Ætius for his disciple or pupil in theology.

Ætius became one of the most conspicuous Arian leaders, although he began life fatherless and in poverty, being some time the slave of a vine-dresser's wife, next a travelling tinker, or goldsmith, then a quack doctor, then a pupil of Paulinus, Arian bishop of Antioch; of Athanasius, of Anazarbus; of Anthony, a priest of Tarsus; and of Leontius, a priest of Antioch. He held disputations with the Gnostics and other sects, practising medicine for a living. Finally he had Eunomius for his pupil and amanuensis (who founded the Eunomian sect), and became at length bishop of Constantinople, where he died, and was buried by Eunomius, being at that time unpopular with the court party. He taught many heretical dogmas, one of which was, that faith alone, without work was sufficient for the salvation of man.

Eunomius, more famous than his master, was a man of great learning and ability. He became bishop of Cyzicum, A.D. 360, but was banished soon after. His Arianism was like that of Ætius — a belief that Christ was a created being, and unlike the Father. Having wandered about much, he died about 394.

Hosius, of Corduba (Cordova), but a native Egyptian, one of the foremost of the Orthodox party, and a chief leader in the Council of Nice, was prevailed upon to sign an Arian creed after that party had banished him in 356, when he was nearly a hundred years of age. He died A.D. 361, having been a bishop more than seventy years.

Meletius did not live long after the council, and upon his death, Alexander resorted to coercive measures in order to bring the Meletians to submission. But they soon joined themselves to his great enemies, the Arians. The Meletian party was still existing in the fifth century.

On page 9, it was stated the Maximian was put to death by order of Constantine. The fact was, he was ordered to commit suicide, or fare worse, and chose to die in that way.

As this history began with Constantine, so it shall end with him. He was probably born at Naissus (now Nissa), in Dacia.

By the divorce of his mother when he was eighteen years old, he was reduced to a state of disgrace and humiliation. Instead then of following his father, he remained in the service of Diocletian, in Egypt and Persia. But his father sent for him just before his death, and Constantine left the palace of Nicomedia in the night to obey the summons. Gibbon further says,— "He ever considered the Council of Nice the bulwark of the Christian faith, and the peculiar glory of his own reign." Constantine's name in Latin is given as "Constantinus, Caius Flavius Valerius Aurelius Claudius." He assumed the titles of Cæsar, Augustus, Victor, and Maximus at different times. His nephew, Julian, was the last emperor of this family.

INDEX

Acesius, bishop of the Novatians, invited to the Council, 91
Achillas, or Achilles, bishop of Alexandria, 28, 37
Admission of women forbidden, 88
Adultery, remark of Constantine upon, 102
Ælia, or Jerusalem, 90
Ætians, 106; See *Eunomians*,
Ætius, originator of the Ætian, or Eunomian sect of Arians, sketch of, 106
Ætius, originator of the Ætian, or Eunomian sect of Arians, sketch of,, 39
Aithalis, or Aithalas, 37
Aix, Council of, 83
Alaphio, 37
Alexander, bishop of Alexandria, 28, 29; dies, 76; letter, 31
Alexander, of Byzantium, 50
Alexandrian Synod, 64
Ambrose, Saint, composes hymns, 64; quoted, 92
Ammonius, father of Arius, 39
Amphion, of Epiphania, 47; and another of Sidon, 47
Anthony of Tarsus, 50
Apion, son of Alexander, 37
Apollinaris, junior, of Antioch, 105
Arian Council, 104
Arian sect, 24
Arian singers, 66
Arians, bent upon establishing their doctrines, 76, 78; favored by Constantine, 51, 63, 104; seventeen bishops at first side with Arius, 79; their arguments reported, 77
Arians, of later times, 24
Arius, another of this name, 38
Arius, originator of Arianism, sketches of him, 28, 104; death of, 29, 104; excommunicated and banished, 63; he writes to Eusebius, of Nicomedia, 38; his creed, 61; his friends, 39; or anathematized, 63; recalled, 104
Armentarius, 10
Arostanes, or Aristens, 47

Athanasius, of Anazarbus, 39, 47, 106
Athanasius, the archbishop of Alexandria, 63; etc, ; quoted, 75, 76, 77; sketches of him, 105; succeeds Alexander, 52
Attig's Hist. Con. Niceni, 67
Augusta, 15
Auxanon, 47

Banquet of Constantine, to which he invites all the bishops, 102
Baronius' Annals of the Church, quoted, 25
Basil, of Amasia, 47, 50
Bethlehem Church, 15
Beveridge's Pandecta Canonum, quoted, 92
Bingham's Antiquities of the Christian Church, quoted, 64
Bishops, known to have attended the Council of Nice, 47; their flattery of the Emperor, 18; their manner of discussion, 53
Boniface III., 31
Books of the Bible, 82
Bower's Lives of the Popes, quoted, 31

Cæcilian, of Carthage, 47
Candidus, the Arian, 66
Canon of Scriptures, 83
Canons of Nice, 67; twenty established, 87
Carpones, 37
Carthage, Council of, 86
Cathari, i. e., the pure (or Puritans), 90
Celibacy, 16, 80
Chlorus, 10, 15
Christ's divine nature, 23
Chrysostom, John, 20
Clarke's Hefele, quoted, 77
Claudia, 10
Coluthus, 32
Conclusion of this history, 106
Confessors present, 47
Constans, son of Constantine, 20

Constantia, sister of Constantine, 18, 20; friendly to Arius, 63

Constantine, his life, 10; baptized, 16; cause of his lenity to Arius, 61; dies, 16; friendly to Acesius, 90; he argues the homoöusian, 77, 79; his army, 17; his character, 18, 23, 96; his cruelty to captives, 18; his daughters, 20; his epistle to absent bishops, 99; his letter to Alexander and Arius, 45; his letters quoted, 66; his Vicennalia and banquet, 102; his will, 21; splendid appearance and speech of, 58

Constantius, son of Constantine, 20

Constantius-Chlorus, 15

Consubstantial Creed, by which party proposed, 63; introduced, and established, 70, 71

Cornelius, bishop of Rome, 91

Council of Nice, causes of its convocation, 27; dates and locality, 25; its objects and results, 24; last day's proceedings, 103; number of bishops present, 50; number of persons present, 47; the discussion, 61; who presided, 56

Council of Nice, the second, 44

Council of Tyre, 75

Council, Arian, prior to the Nicene, 104; of Antioch, 104

Councils of various times and places, 24

Creed of the orthodox party, 85; Arian rejected, 61; confirmed by decree of Constantine, 94

Crispus, son of Constantine, 18, 19, 20

Cyclopædia, New American, quoted, 71

Cynon, 50

Dachius, of Berenice, 50

Dalmatius, 19, 20

Day of Rest, 6

Daza, 13

Deacons, their duties, 94

Desios, (Lat. Desius), the Greek name of the month of June, 50

Diocletian, 10

Dionysius, bishop of Rome, 78

Divine nature of Christ, 29

Doctrines and discipline., See Canons

Domnus, of Stridon, 47

Dying penitents, 93

Easter, the day on which Christ's, resurrection is commemorated, called also Paschal Feast, festival, or solemnity, first instituted A. D. 68, 86, 99

Ecclesiastes, quoted, 9

Epilogue, 105

Epiphanius, his account of heresies quoted, 28; etc., ; sketch of, 82

Eucharist, 94

Eulalius, 47

Eunomius, the acute theologian, and founder of a sect of Arians, 106

Eupsychius, of Tyana, 47, 51

Eusebians, i. e., Arians, 105

Eusebius Pamphilus, or Pamphili, bishop of Cæsarea, 42, 55; his letter quoted, 86; his letter to Alexander, 10, 19, 36; of, 51; sketch creed, 69; subscribes the Nicene creed, 72

Eusebius, of Nicomedia, 19, 20, 63; baptizes Constantine, 16, 52; defends and support Arius, 52; his letter to Paulinus, bishop of Tyre, 41; sketch of, 53, 105; the Arians, called also Eusebians, propound their doctrines, 53

Eustathius, bishop of Antioch, 47, 60; quoted, 64, 75; sketch of, 74

Eustorgius, 50

Eutropius, 10

Eutychius, 50

Euzoius, 37

Fabianus, bishop of Rome, 90

Fausta, 13, 18, 20

Formulary, or confession of faith, 85;
    of Eusebius Pamphilus, 70. See,
    also, *Creed*

Gaius, 38
Galerius, 10, 11, 13
Gallus, 19
Garden of Eden, 7
Gibbons's Decline and Fall of the
    Roman Empire, quoted, 18, 19,
    20, 21, 40, 107
Gratian, 20
Gregory, of Berytus, which was
    anciently "Beroe," and is now
    Beirout, and the name "Berea,"
    given in Theodoret, should
    probably be Beroe, 39, 50
Gregory, of Cæsarea, quoted, 56

Hadrian, or Adrian , pope of Rome,
    quoted, 51
Hagiographa, 82
Hammond's, Canons, quoted, 67
Hannibalianus, 19
Harpocration, 50
Hefele quoted, 76, 86
Helena, 10, 15, 20, 22
Hell, 9
Helladius, 38
Hellanicus, 39
Hermogenes, 50
Hilary, ecclesiastical historian,
    quoted, 51
Hippo, Council of, 86
Holy Sepulchre, 15
Homoiousios, introduced by the
    Arians, 61
Homoöusian, the, 63, 64; explained
    by Constantine, 80
Homoöusian, the word introduced by
    the Orthodox, 63, 64, 86
Hosius, or Osius, bishop of Corduba
    (Cordova), 22, 23, 44, 56, 106;
    sketch of him, 106
Huxley, 8
Hymn to God, 86
Hymns, first composed by Arius, St.
    Ambrose, Victorinus, etc., 64;

one to God, decreed by the
    Council, 86
Hypatius, of Gangra, 51

Introduction, 5

Jews, their Passover, 23, 86, 99
Job, 8
Judith, book of, 82
Julian, the emperor, 18, 19, 20
Julius, 37
Julius Constantius, 19
Justin Martyr, quoted, 94

Kneeling at prayers, 94

Labarum, 12, 13
Laodicea, Council of, 82
Lapsed Presbyters, 93; catechumens,
    93
Lardner, Dr., quoted, 25
Lateran Palace, 13
Leontius, bishop, a eunuch, 50, 87
Letter, of Alexander, bishop of
    Alexandria, concerning Arius,
    31; of Arius, 39; of Constantine,
    67; of Eusebius Pamphilus, 70;
    of Eusebius, of Nicomedia, 41;
    others of Constantine, quoted,
    99
Licinius, 13, 14, 18, 27, 46
Licinius, son of Licinius, 21
Longinus, of Cappodocia, 51
Longinus, of Pontus, 51
Lord's Day made legal Sunday, 16
Lucian, of Antioch, 104
Lucius, 37
Luther, Martin, quoted, 85

Macarius, 39, 50
Macedonius, 105
Mansi, quoted, 47
Marcellinus, 31
Marcellinus, of Ancyra, 50
Marcellus, of Ancyra, 105
Marcus Aurelius, 22
Marcus, of Calabria, 50
Maris, the Arian, 51, 63

Maronite, 66
Martial, the poet, quoted, 66
Martyr, Justin, quoted, 94
Mary, "mother of God,", 37
Maxentius, 12
Maximian, 10, 13, 14, 18
Maximin, 14, 27, 82
Meletians, 23, 80
Meletius, of Lycus, and his followers, 50
Meletius, of Pontus, 50
Melitius, of Lycus, and his followers, 80
Menas, or Minas, 37
Menophantus sides with Arius, 60
Mexia, quoted, 5
Mill, J. S., quoted, 18
Miltiades, or Melchiades, 31
Minervina, 10, 19
Miracles, performers of, present, 51, 53
Moses, 8, 9
Mosheim's Institute, quoted, 26
Mount of Olives Church, 15
Murdock, Dr. James, quoted, 26

Narcissus, the Arian, 50, 60
Neander, ecclesiastical historian, quoted, 26
Nero mentioned, 22
Nicasius, 50
Nice, its ancient and modern names, 45
Nicholas, of Myra, 50
Novations, 25; re-admitted to communion, 90
Novatus, or Novatian, and his sect, 90; quoted, 91
Number of bishops present, 51

Objects of the Council, 23
Ordination of bishops, 89
Origen, 9
Orthodox faith., (See *Nicene Creed*, *Homoöusian*, etc

Pagi, Dr. Anthony, editor of Baronius, quoted, 58

Pamphylus, or Pamphilus , the martyr, 51
Paphnutius, of Egypt, 46, 51; being a confessor, his wounds kissed by the emperor, 101; favors marriage, 80
Parties present, 51
Passover, or Paschal feast, 23, 86
Pastor, book of the, quoted, 77
Patrophilus, the Arian, 50
Paul, 12 years old, 50
Paul, of Neo-Cæsarea, a confessor, 50
Paul, of Samosata, 94
Paulinus and Julian, consuls of Rome, 25, 50
Paulinus, bishop of Antioch, 50
Paulinus, Bishop of Tyre, 39, 41
Penitent, a dying one, 93
Persecutions by the Roman emperors, 45
Petavius, Dionysius, editor of Epiphanius, quoted, 29, 31
Peter, bishop of Alexandria, a martyr, 27, 28, 82
Philogonius, 38, 39
Philostorgius, ecclesiastical historian, sketch of him, 40, 64; quoted, 40
Photinus, of Sirmium, 105
Pistus, of Athens, 50
Plato and his logos, 17
Platonism, 29, 105
Pope, 31; (a title first adopted at Rome, by Hygenus, A. D. 138), supremacy of the Roman, 31
Potamon, of Heraclea, 51
Presidents of the Council, 57
Primacy of certain churches, 89
Protogenes, 51
purgatory, 9

Quarrels of the bishops settled by Constantine, 59

Roman pope, 31, 91
Rufinus, ecclesiastical historian, quoted, 51, 79

Sabbath, 15

Sabellianism, 28, 105
Sarmatis, 37
Schisms., See *Arians*, *Meletians*, *Novations*, *Eunomians*, etc
Schlegel, J. R., quoted, 21
Second marriage, 92
Secundus, the Arian, 50; anathematized, 61; excommunicated, 79
Self-mutilators, proscribed, 87
Sentianus, 51
Sibyls, as true predictors, 17
Silvester, bishop, or pope, of Rome, 13, 31
Socrates, Scholasticus, ecclesiastical historian, sketch of him, 25; quoted, 44
Socrates, the philosopher, 17
Solomon, king, 9
Sotadés, a poet, 66
Sozomen, ecclesiastical historian, sketch of him, 37; quoted, 53, 80, 90, 102
Spyridon, 50, 51, 53
Stanley, A. P., dean of Westminster, quoted, 16, 18, 19, 22
Sunday instituted, 15
Symbol (see *Creed* and *Formulary*), 85
Synod, (See *Council*)
Synodical epistle, 96
Synodicon, of Athanasius, 50

Tarcodinatus, 51
Thalia, 61; quoted, 61, 77
Theodora, 15
Theodore, of Mopsuestia, quoted, 57
Theodoret, ecclesiastical historian, sketch of him, 27; quoted, 27
Theodotius, 39
Theodotus, 36
Theognis, the Arian, 50; banished, 63
Theonas, the Arian, 51, 63; excommunicated, 61
Theophilus, 51
Tillemont's Hist. of Rome, 104
Translation to new Sees forbidden, 93
Trinity dogma, its origin, etc., 29 See *Plato*,
Tryphillius, 51

Tyndall, 8
Tyre, Council of, 76

Usury forbidden, 93

Valeria, 10
Valerius, 10
Valesius, Henry, ecclesiastical historian, quoted, 51
Vicennalia, of Constantine, 102
Victorinus, Fabius Marius, the rhetorician, quoted, 51, 67
Vincent, of Rome, 53
Virgil, quoted, 17
Vito, or Victor, 51

Walford, Edward, A.M., translator of Socrates, Philostorgius, etc., 27
Women not to be *Sorores*, 88

Young, Edward, poet, 9

Zenobia, queen of Palmyra, 97
Zophyrus, 50
Zosimus, quoted, 23

SELECTED TITLES
A&B Publishers Group

African Discovery of America	10.00
Aids the End of Civilization	9.95
Anacalypsis (set)	45.00
Anacalypsis Vol. 1	25.00
Anacalypsis Vol. 11	20.00
Arab Invasion of Egypt	14.95
Blackmen Say Goodbye to Misery	10.00
Columbus & the African Holocaust	10.00
Columbus Conspiracy	11.95
Dawn Voyage	11.95
Education of the Negro	9.95
First Council of Nice	9.95
Gospel of Barnabas	8.95
Gerald Massey's Lectures	9.95
Heal Thyself	9.95
Heal Thyself Cookbook	9.95
Historical Jesus & the Mythical Christ	9.95
Harlem Voices	11.95
Harlem USA	11.95
Lost Books of the Bible	9.95
Vaccines are Dangerous	9.95

Send for our complete catalog now

Mail Order Form to **A&B PUBLISHERS GROUP · 1000 ATLANTIC AVE · BROOKLYN · NEW YORK · 11238**
TEL: (718) 783-7808· FAX (718) 783-7267

Name:_____

Address_____

City_____ST_____Zip_____

Card Type_____

Card Number_____Exp_____/_____

Signature _____

We accept VISA MASTERCARD AMERICAN EXPRESS & DISCOVER